BOATING® MAGAZINE'S

INSIDER'S GUIDE

to

BUYING A

POWERBOAT

J. P. Lamy

International Marine / McGraw-Hill

Camden, Maine • New York • San Francisco • Washington, D.C. • Auckland • Bogotá
Caracas • Lisbon • London • Madrid • Mexico City • Milan • Montreal • New Delhi
San Juan • Singapore • Sydney • Tokyo • Toronto

**To Debbie and Tommy J . . .
for believing**

International Marine
A Division of The **McGraw-Hill** Companies

10 9 8 7 6 5 4
Copyright © 2000 Robert J. P. Lamy
All rights reserved. The publisher takes no responsibility for the use of any of the materials
or methods described in this book, nor for the products thereof. The name "International Marine"
and the International Marine logo are trademarks of The McGraw-Hill Companies.
Printed in the United States of America.

Boating® is a registered trademark of Hachette Filipacchi Magazines, Inc.,
used under license by International Marine.

Library of Congress Cataloging-in-Publication Data
Lamy, J. P.
    Boating magazine's insider's guide to buying a powerboat / J. P. Lamy.
        p.   cm.
    Includes index.
    ISBN 0-07-135150-7
    1. Motorboats—Purchasing—United States.   I. Title.
VM341.L35   1999
623.8'231'0296—dc21   99-042564
                                        CIP

Questions regarding the content of this book should be addressed to
International Marine
P.O. Box 220
Camden, ME 04843
www.internationalmarine.com

Questions regarding the ordering of this book should be addressed to
The McGraw-Hill Companies
Customer Service Department
P.O. Box 547
Blacklick, OH 43004
Retail customers: 1-800-262-4729
Bookstores: 1-800-722-4726

This book is printed on 55-lb. Sebago

Printed by R. R. Donnelley & Sons, Crawfordsville, IN
Design by Carol Gillette, Communication Graphics
Production by Archetype and Dan Kirchoff
Edited by Jonathan Eaton, Alex Barnett, and Cynthia Flanagan Goss

Contents

Preface

Why go boating? That is probably the easiest question I'll answer in this book. Who doesn't remember their first visit to the water? Standing there with the sand warm between your toes, mesmerized by the rhythmic sounds and movement of the waves. The excitement of seeing the fish jump, arching silently over the water, splashing gracefully back in, inviting you to join them for a swim. Who hasn't wondered what life lies below the waves? What lies beyond the horizon?

Purchasing a boat is one of the most important lifestyle decisions you will make. This decision will affect the enjoyment of your hard-earned leisure time. It should, therefore, be approached as seriously as any other major purchase, such as your home and your car. The biggest question is, after all, how much do you value your time and money? If you are like me, the value is very high.

This pocket guide will give you all the tools you need to find the best deal on a new or used boat and save thousands of dollars. Whether you're dealing with a boatowner or an experienced boat salesperson, you'll be able to approach all aspects of the sales process with con-fidence. You'll be in charge of the moment. The boat you buy will be the one of your choosing, on your terms. Together, we'll put the fun back into boat shopping, where it belongs!

PART 1
First Things

In 1987 I started a business buying small used power-boats, fixing them up, and reselling them at profit. Over the years I have purchased hundreds of used boats, both for resale and for my own use. With a few exceptions I have always found great deals. In 1994 I began selling new powerboats as well.

It's easier than you think to find a good boat and then negotiate honestly to get it at the right price, the first time. That notion was the seed for this book.

This pocket guide originally began as an overview for a business venture in which I'd hoped to help the first-time boat buyer buy the right boat, at the best price, the first time. After a few days' work, I realized one person would be able to do very little to offset the odds stacked against buyers in general. As this outline progressed, it occurred to me that I should forget the business venture and send this message to buyers nationwide.

This guide will show you, step by step, how to choose the right size and type of boat to suit your wants and needs. A boat you do not really like is never a bargain, no matter how attractive the price. First, we'll briefly cover how boats are built and thereby learn how to recognize quality. Then, I'll explain the basic boat types available and provide a questionnaire that you and your family can use to find the type that best suits your needs.

We'll then take a fun and informative journey into the realm of boat researching and purchasing. We will cover every aspect of the purchase, from inspecting and pricing boats to dealing with the individual seller or professional salesperson. You'll be equipped with a boat inspection checklist, simple yet effective negotiating tips, and even financing secrets no banker would want you to know!

At times it may seem that our inspection and negotiating techniques, while honest, are taking advantage of the seller. This is not so. We are merely trying to level the playing field in a world that often operates by the slogan, "Let the buyer beware!" Most folks want to be honest, but it's rare that a seller will disclose all the negative features of his boat. He may need the money badly. Perhaps the cost of maintenance and repair is beyond his means. Some fast-talking sales manager may have talked him into more boat than he could really afford. (I think of the lyrics of an old song by Traffic: "And the man in the suit has just bought a new car with the profit he's made on your dreams.")

Whatever the reason, it's typically the buyer that will get the short end of the stick. Our system will effectively even the odds for you.

My intention is that this guide will open eyes in the boating industry. There has been a lot of talk in recent years in the boating press about how frequently first-time boat buyers are getting substandard products and services, and consequently turning to some other form of recreation. This industry needs stricter pricing regulation, higher standards of safety, and increased education for the boatowner and operator if it is to prosper and grow. I hope this book enhances your own education and helps you in your search for the best deal on a new or used powerboat.

1
Buying New or Used

Whether to buy new or used, that is the primary question. This is not always a question of disposable income, I assure you. Sometimes a great deal on a used boat can bring more pleasure than the new-smelling, brightly untouched polish of the new factory product. You should decide in advance which you're seeking. A good way to begin is to list the pros and cons of new and used boats and take the time to fully evaluate your wants and needs. Here are some immediate considerations.

New

- ▣ **Warranties.** A new boat will have a comprehensive manufacturer's warranty covering all structural and electrical systems. A warranty will cover at least the first year. Get a written copy of the warranty and actually read it.

- ▣ **Condition.** A new boat should be in pristine condition, free from blemish or defect.

- ▣ **Customized options.** You may equip your new boat with electronics, seating, canvas, and so forth to suit.

- ▣ **Brand name.** You can pick from your favorite manufacturers and models, and your decision does not have to be determined by what is available on the used-boat market for only a short period of time.

- ▣ **No hidden surprises.** Having never been used, all systems and features of a new boat will be in their original configuration and working order—and will never have been exposed to the ministrations of some backwoods mechanic.

▣ **Proper match of boat and power.** The Coast Guard requires boat-builders to post a maximum horsepower rating on all out-board-powered boats under 20 feet in length (see sidebar on capacity plates, page 35). Many manufacturers volun-tarily provide horsepower ratings on larger boats and boats powered by inboards or inboard/outboards. You should aim for 80 to 100 percent of the maximum power rating to ensure satisfactory performance and protect the resale value. Buying new allows you to do this. It's not unusual to see boats, both new and used, that are underpowered in an effort to hold down the price of the whole package. It's not worth it. The motor may seem adequate with one or two aboard. But the boat may perform and handle poorly with a full crew. An underpowered boat is also likely to disappoint you when you want to resell it.

Used

▣ **Lower price, lower payments.** A smaller initial investment should net you smaller payments. As a rule, a new vessel depreciates significantly in the first two to three years. This is generally the result of overpayment in the first place—something we are here to avoid.

▣ **Easier to resell.** I've always maintained that I make my money when I buy a boat, not when I sell it. Buying a boat at the right price will make your task of reselling down the road much easier.

▣ **Possible profit.** The profit potential of the right used boat is what got me started, with very little knowledge or money. Watch yourself, however: it's easy to overlook some of the steps to buying a powerboat and leave your-self exposed to a profit-eating repair bill.

▣ **Accessories come with the boat.** If you're lucky and astute, you may come home with a fully or partially equipped boat,

Underpowered, Overpowered

Years ago, when I was selling boats for my first marina, I conducted a sea trial with a family of five very large people. The boat in question was a 21-foot cuddy/cruiser on consignment, powered by a 4-cylinder, 135-hp inboard/outboard. To my dismay, after 30 or 45 seconds of running at full throttle, I couldn't get the boat on a plane. Eventually I had to ask the father and son to move as far forward as possible. They purchased the boat but were never very happy with the performance.

At the other end of the spectrum, I remember a 17-foot center console with a 140-hp outboard that I'd purchased through a marina in a package deal. I had a buyer before I'd even had a chance to splash the boat.

We put the boat in the water for the first time together, and it ran out fine, extremely fast. It was a lot of motor for that boat, so when we pulled up to the dock—me standing on the bow—I looked back to make sure the boat wasn't taking on water through the scuppers. What I didn't realize at the time was that my weight at the bow had raised the stern just enough to keep the scuppers above water.

After returning from the tag office, the new owner and I found the boat with about a foot of water inside. After pumping out the boat and plugging the scuppers, he still liked the deal enough to keep the boat (and the scupper plugs). When in doubt, always check the scuppers at the dock.

saving further expenditures for anchor, lines, life jackets, fenders, flares, foghorn, compass, depth sounder, and other required or advisable items (see appendix 4, Coast Guard–Required Safety Gear).

☐ **Money left for new roof.** This one should be self-explanatory: the money you save buying a used boat can be put toward repairs and upgrades. However, don't bet the farm, or you may end up living on a 19-foot cuddy-cabin boat. Not a pretty thought.

If you're like me, you may take a long time to come to this first decision—new or used. If you decide to go for a used boat, you should follow that course deliberately. To jump from used to new out of frustration will definitely cost you money and usually cost you your ability to deal effectively. I've seen some pretty savvy buyers fold like a cheap tent after weeks of frustration and leap at an overpriced new boat just to "get it over with." As we shall see, you should always try to leave your emotions at home.

TRAP

Avoid underpowered outboard boats—both performance and resale will suffer.

Boat shopping should be great fun. So often we lose sight of this and ruin the whole process. Boating is a recreational activity. There are many ways to begin the buying process. I like the local newspaper classifieds, *Boat Trader* and similar trader magazines (regional publications featuring grainy photos and brief descriptions that you can find in convenience stores, newsstands, and marine stores), and even local shopping guides. Are you hooked into the Internet? If so, you can access all the local newspaper classifieds in one sitting. Better yet, check out my favorite boating website, Trader Online *<http://www.traderonline.com/>*. You can narrow a nationwide database of classified ads with customized search criteria, get some great pricing information, and never leave your favorite chair (food and beverage breaks notwithstanding).

TRAP

Don't throw yourself at a new boat out of frustration with your search for a used boat. The impatient buyer always pays too much.

Once you have found some interesting targets online, go to the N.A.D.A. (National Automotive Dealers Association) Appraisal Guide site *<http://www.nadaguides.com/>*. This is an Internet version of the legendary industry pricing guide for used boats and motors. Just follow the instructions (even I was able to find my way around) to research your year, make, and model. I will be saying more about the Internet and pricing guides in later chapters.

Although a professional survey—an inspection conducted by an experienced marine surveyor—can be a terrific tool, I find that with smaller boats (under 25 feet) they are not very cost effective. Additionally, surveyors worth their salt are booked for weeks in advance. Spending around $300 per boat until you find the right one can more than offset the money you'd hope to save by buying a used boat. We cover the boat inspection process thoroughly in later chapters and always recommend hiring a mechanic prior to purchase.

In this book you will find two separate sections dealing with the process of boat shopping—one for used boats and one for new. But the sections are often interrelated and are most effective when used together. If you're looking at used boats, for instance, the new-boat inspection checklist can be a very handy tool when coupled with the inspection checklist for used boats. Try it and see. The next section, Boatbuilding 101, will provide you with the basic tools for understanding how a boat is built and what to look for when shopping. Happy hunting!

Boatbuilding 101: What You Don't See

You will need to take your time with this chapter, for what we need to do here is cover, in general terms, what goes into building the hull of a fiberglass powerboat. It's good to at least know the basics, for those moments when that salesperson is telling you that the wavy hull you're staring down is perfectly normal.

The building process starts with a female mold, the inside surface of which (like the inside of a cereal bowl) is polished to a mirrorlike finish. A technician first applies the gelcoat, hand spraying it over the entire inside surface of the mold. The gelcoat, which is pigmented polyester resin, will eventually become that glossy colored finish you see on the exterior of your boat. Industry standard gelcoat thickness is 22 mils, or 22 thousandths of an inch. Too little or too much can result in stress cracks—hairline cracks resembling spider webs—that on a new boat are the first sign of substandard manufacturing. Poor-quality gelcoat will result in chalking, discoloration, and moisture penetration. If this is accompanied by resin voids or other defects in the first layer of fiberglass under the gelcoat, the result could be boat pox (bubbles or blisters in the gelcoat). If you see discoloration or blisters on a new model, run away! These can be temporarily fixed, but there is no long-term cure short of peeling the entire layer of gelcoat. Once applied, this gelcoat layer should then be allowed to set up completely.

Next comes the first layer of fiberglass, which is crucial to the entire structural integrity of the hull. In standard practice the first layer is chopped-strand mat, a coarse mat of short fibers adhered to a textile scrim in random directions. Our technician will apply the mat by hand and carefully roll it out with resin onto the gelcoat layer. A cheaper and faster way to accomplish this is by use of a chopper gun. Here the fiberglass strands are literally chopped up, mixed with resin, and shot onto the gelcoat layer in one continuous operation. This can lead to uneven layers, weak spots, and hot spots (an area where too much resin pools and cures incorrectly) and usually results in a less-than-desirable finished product. Fortunately, chopper gun application is less and less common, but mats all look alike on the outside. If you're buying a new boat, ask about this. If you're buying a used boat, a call to the manufacturer should tell you whether it was hand laid or built with a chopper gun. If you can't find out, you can still make inferences from the other indications of quality.

A good builder spends a great deal of time here, hand-rolling out any excess resin to avoid bubbles or hot spots. Ideally, the entire mold is gimbaled to roll the boat in a 180-degree arc so that no resin may pool in the low spots. (This also gives the laminators full access to the work surface while standing outside the mold.) This layer is then allowed to harden and begin cooling.

The next step to ensure a quality product is to fill in the strakes—the fin-like extrusions that run from stem to stern below the waterline—to strengthen them and present a flat interior bonding surface for subsequent layers of fiberglass. This is done with a microballoon putty, a heavy fiberglass resin mixed with tiny silicon microballoons in paste form. The putty is then allowed to harden and begin cooling.

I mention hardening and cooling because timing is crucial in fiberglass construction. As the resin cures it releases heat. If successive layers of fiberglass and resin are applied too quickly, the layup will become too hot, producing warping and those wavy hull surfaces we aim to avoid. If it cools too much between applications, the layers may not adhere to each other properly.

Cheaper and Faster

The new 21-foot center console was powered by a 150-hp outboard and was very fast. The new owner was out in the Gulf of Mexico, flying along at top speed, when the entire center console flipped back on top of him. There he was, doing about 50 mph and unable to work the steering or throttle controls. Luckily he remembered to yank the kill switch lanyard, which turned off the motor. Being out in the Gulf, he had lots of room to slow down. He did manage to get the boat back (somewhat slower, I'd imagine). Be cautious with really inexpensive brands.

Next there are usually at least three more layers of fiberglass, which are again hand applied. A typical fiberglass hull is composed of alternating layers of chopped-strand mat and woven roving, a thicker fabric of flat fiberglass strands woven together in a grid pattern. To reduce weight, some manufacturers are beginning to substitute a multilayer roving for multiple layers of conventional woven roving. For example, a biaxial roving consists of two layers, with the strands in the upper layer all oriented at 90 degrees to the one beneath. A triaxial roving adds a third layer with strands oriented on the bias. The innermost layer is usually mat, or sometimes fiberglass cloth (which resembles woven roving but has a lighter, finer weave), for a reasonably smooth finish. The boat is hopefully still in the mold at this time. In the rush to increase production without increasing the number of additional molds, some well known manufacturers will pop the boat out of the mold as quickly as possible to start the next unit, which sometimes results in distortion of the finished hull.

The next step is the installation of the stringer system and wire channels. The stringers nowadays usually consist of a molded one-piece fiberglass grid system made to strengthen the hull and support the deck. But stringers can be made of wood or fiberglass. Each has its advantages and characteristics; I do not have a preference except to say that I prefer a proper installation.

The boat should be still in the mold at this point. If wood stringers are used, a good marine fir is preferable. Properly resined wood stringers that are completely and properly encapsulated with fiberglass mat or cloth will produce an excellent product; fir is a dry wood and will impregnate nicely with resin, unlike a marine plywood. Installation of either system should include microballoon putty on all contact surfaces with the hull (and eventually the cockpit) to soften the edges and corners and prevent air bubbles in the overlying fiberglass. The entire grid is then attached with hand-rolled fiberglass mat or cloth to the hull. The transom core—usually thick wood or, more recently, dense urethane foam—is installed at the same time and encased in laminate. The finished product is now structurally one unit—what boatbuilders call a *monocoque* structure.

Our crew will next install the fuel tank, prewire the boat, and clear the water passages (the bilge). There are two ways to finish off a boat at this point. The less expensive method is to build the cockpit floor and any elevated deck spaces (sidedecks, foredeck, casting deck) piecemeal.

In this case, the cockpit floor is usually wood. More recently, however, fiberglass cored with high-density foam has been used. This process produces what I call, for want of a better word, a "skiff"-type boat, the characteristic feature of which is the inside surface of the hull visible above the floor. The gunwale (pronounced *gunn'l*) is created where the top edge of the hull curls outward and down. The rubrail attaches directly to this overhang in the hull, and the fasteners are usually exposed underneath. The interiors of such boats are generally not as nicely finished, and wooden decks are more susceptible to warping and rot down the line. Not my favorite application.

The preferable method is to create a fiberglass hull liner that incorporates the cockpit "tub" and deck spaces in a single unit, and then mate it with the hull. Like the hull, the liner unit is fabricated in a mold and can be reproduced flawlessly. Walking surfaces are cored with wood or high-density foam for strength and stiffness and have a gelcoat finish. Backing plates should be preinstalled on the inside of the liner wherever cleats and high-load fixtures will go. The liner normally wraps over the top edge of the hull, creating a vertical overlap of an inch or more. The rubrail attaches on the outside of this seam with fasteners that sandwich the rubrail, liner, and hull in a single joint. The builder should use stainless steel screws every 6 inches, install a backing material (often wood strips) on the inside of the hull to receive the screws, and apply a layer of sealant to the hull-liner joint.

Finally, in either approach, a high-density, closed-cell foam is injected into the dead spaces beneath the flooring or liner, which upon curing provides flotation, additional hull rigidity, and sound insulation. Another advantage of the hull-liner method is that the foam can be made to extend well up into the hull wall, providing additional buoyancy.

Obviously, there is quite a bit more to the finished product than I have mentioned here. But the rest of the boat should be readily accessible for your inspection. Please mark this chapter. We'll be referring back to it when we come to the inspection phase of the boat purchase. A general understanding of how a quality boat is constructed will be a great help as we try to separate the good, the bad, and the ugly.

Boat Types and Their Primary Uses

First, let's sketch out the different hull types. Almost every hull we'll be discussing will be made of fiberglass. A flotation or nonplaning hull—such as a sailboat, pontoon boat, or large ship—must be pushed through the water and is limited in speed because of the larger area of wetted surface plowing through the water. As a rule it takes a lot of power to move a nonplaning hull at any kind of speed. The major exception is the catamaran, which has two smaller hulls and presents less resistance, or wetted surface.

The more popular hull type for powerboats, and the one we'll be dealing with for the most part, is a planing hull. This design actually gets up on top of the water at speed and outruns its bow wake. I'm sure you've seen fast-moving boats with the bow up in the air, contacting the water amidships (about center) or even farther back. The boat starts out slowly, and as the speed increases the bow points high. But then you feel the bow start to sink (poor choice of words, I know) and speed radically increases. Now you're up on plane.

The way a boat rides is primarily determined by its deadrise, or its angle of V. The bow deadrise may be flat or sharp, from a virtual 0 to 50 degrees or better. The sharper the V here, the better a boat will slice through the waves at speed. It is the angle of deadrise at the transom (or stern) that most affects the ride of the boat.

Picture yourself coming across the wake of a 46-foot sportfish in a narrow channel at about 20 or 25 mph (a slower planing speed). You go over the first wave all right, but you land on the second one amidships. The angle of V there will determine if you land softly (with a deeper V slicing through the wave) or hit hard (with a modified or flatter V)—and wish you'd brought that kidney belt! When you're planing, your sharp bow will only cut through a wave if you're pointing down.

Your primary choices are deep V or modified V, which is determined at the transom. There are advantages and disadvantages to each.

A typical modified V has the sharp entry of a V hull at the bow but flattens out to a deadrise of 20 degrees or less at the transom. This presents a flatter surface to the water. Modified V hulls have advantages: they can operate in shallower water, they have better side-to-side stability, they will achieve faster speeds, and they are easier to plane and generally have a drier ride. Sounds like a lot of pluses, right? On a smaller boat, say under 21 feet, the modified V has a lot going for it. The major disadvantage is a bumpy ride in choppy water and ocean swells.

A hull with 22 degrees or more deadrise at the transom is thought of as deep V. (Don't ask me where 21 degrees ends up; I'm as lost as you are there!) This doesn't sound like much difference, I know, but the difference in ride is noticeable. The main advantages of the deep V are a smoother ride, particularly in the ocean swells, and marginally better cornering. The disadvantages are a tendency to be a little "tender" side to side, a wetter ride, a longer time to get up on plane, and a deeper draft.

You can probably decide what degree of V suits your needs by thinking about where you're likely to spend most of your time. If you plan to use the boat primarily in protected bays or on rivers and lakes, the modified V is best—large boat wakes notwithstanding. I wouldn't get a flat-bottom boat unless you need to operate in ankle-deep water; a deadrise of 18 or 20 degrees should cover you for about 95 percent of your operating needs.

An avid offshore boater will need a deep V. It's much better to be a little tender side to side and a little wetter than to slam your way to the Bahamas. A deep V ride at speed in the ocean swells is one of the most exhilarating experiences one can have.

Now, on to the different types of boats.

If you're a first-time buyer (or second, or third), this section will be of special interest to you. I cover as much ground as possible to help you in your choice of boat types. For the purposes of this book, I talk about powerboats 30 feet and under, although in truth, a lot of techniques discussed in later chapters will help all boat buyers. I cover uses, advantages, and disadvantages of each of the 14 basic boat types.

1. Center Console

The center console is the all-around favorite of fair-weather fishermen everywhere. I know you've seen it:

Center console. (Photograph of 220 Sportsman courtesy of Pro-Line Boats)

a very seaworthy-looking vessel with a large open bow
area, a center steering station, and lots of room from bow
to stern for fishing and diving. They are generally armed
to the teeth for battling fish, with live baitwells, fish storage boxes, outriggers, fishing rod holders, and electronics.
They come as small as 13 feet and get as large as 45 feet.

As I've mentioned, a modified V hull is great up to
around 21 feet, but anything larger should go to a deep V
hull to allow the option of offshore fishing. Center console boats are mostly powered by outboards, either single
or twin, but I have seen some great inboard-powered center consoles. When properly set up, these are roomy and
fuel efficient. But if you want speed, stick with outboards.
Inboard/outboard models (otherwise known as stern-
drive) are also fuel efficient, but they tend to take up a lot
of your rear cockpit fishing space. These are quite possibly
the least desirable of the three engine options.

The center console is a versatile boat. The forward
casting platform can provide seating for two to four people. There is usually seating on the front of the console,
and rear seating is available on some models. The design is
open, so unless it's decked out in cumbersome canvas, the

boat offers no place to hide when bad weather hits. Not surprisingly, these are much more popular in the southern states. Some larger models have enclosed heads in the console or even a forward cuddy cabin.

The center consoles are also good for watersports. With the proper power, they can tow skiers, tubers, or kneeboarders—whatever your pleasure. Smaller center consoles have limited storage, so your equipment may have to remain on deck when not in use. Decks are gel-coated fiberglass, use no carpet, and have little excess cushioning. This makes them great for easy clean-up and storing out in the elements. Except in the smallest versions (under 15 feet), these boats are normally self-bailing and any water taken on will drain overboard without pumping. This is critical if you intend to store the boat in a wet slip. Self-bailing or not, the boat should always have a working bilge pump aboard.

2. Flats Boats

Flats boat. (Photograph of 183 Sport courtesy of Pro-Line Boats)

A newer version of the center console, a flats boat is generally low in profile, has a wide beam, and is powered to the maximum with an outboard motor. Think of it as a saltwater fisherman's bass boat. Flat boats typically have a nonskid gunwale (top of the hull wall) wide enough to walk around without stepping down into the cockpit deck. Like center consoles, these are armed to the teeth with fishing rod holders, live baitwells, fish storage boxes, and even built-in fishing tackle boxes.

These boats cater to the flats and the fly fishing crews that explore the salt- or freshwater backwater territories. They are designed to operate in very shallow waters, typically less than 1 foot (bring a spare prop). Flats boats are almost always modified V hulls. The deck and gunwale areas have little or no unnecessary obstructions to trip you up. Deck cleats and lights are usually recessed or pop up when needed. The idea is to be able to fish 360 degrees around the boat while fly casting with no entanglements for feet or fishing line.

Flats boat designs are well thought out for the dedicated shallow water anglers. Many are equipped with a trolling motor (a virtually silent electric motor mounted on the bow for small maneuvers near your favorite fishing hole). Some even have a poling platform on the stern, which allows you to pole the boat silently into the shallowest of water to approach your target without spooking the fish. Even the low profile of the boat serves this purpose, so as not to cast a shadow that will alert your prey. Yes, some good polarized sunglasses and sharp eyes actually allow you to spot the fish lying just below the surface. Then a well-practiced cast will land your lure just ahead of that hungry redfish.

Please note that I do not recommend flats boats for family use. They usually do not offer the safety of higher gunwales (sidewalls), bow rails, and secure seating one would want for keeping children aboard. Foul weather and wind protection is virtually nonexistent. As with the bass boat, a bimini top is almost never an option.

3. Walk-around Cuddy

Walk-around cuddy. (Photograph of 221 Walk-around courtesy of Pro-Line Boats)

This is another favorite deck design for fishing and diving. A standard model would have lots of fishing gear and features, a large rear cockpit, and limited seating. Walk-around cuddies are great when the weather turns bad: you can go below to the cabin or hide under a canvas top and behind the wraparound windshield. The forward cabin design blocks wind and waves and can house your children, your gear, your bathroom, even yourselves. Nicer models have screened, opening portholes and a forward access hatch. Once again, a modified V hull is great up to around 21 feet, but anything larger should go to a deep V hull to allow the option of offshore fishing.

The walk-around cuddies are typically powered by outboards or inboard/outboards. Larger models may go to inboards.

Outboards will give you the most cockpit space and the best speed, but they are the least fuel efficient. For saltwater applications they are the engine of choice, followed by inboards. Inboard/outboards are fast and fuel efficient, but salt water wreaks havoc on them. They are also the hardest to maintain.

The design is user-friendly and allows 360-degree access around the cabin in relative safety, particularly in larger seas. It's best to actually take this walk before buying (the smaller models have smaller walkways). Be sure the boat you pick is safe for you and your crew. Rails need to be strong and secure: they may be the only thing between you and an unexpected swim.

This design is one of my favorites. I usually make up for the lack of rear seats with some stout deck chairs. The hulls and decks are usually all fiberglass without carpet and are easy to maintain. The design lends itself to almost any watersport. You can store your waterskiing gear down below and then go right to your favorite fishing spot. Additionally, these boats are almost always self-bailing. I recommend 20 feet in length or more, as anything smaller tends to be topheavy and may handle poorly.

4. Dual Console

A dual console is a nice compromise between the interests of fishing and family. The dual console has a bowrider-like configuration with a split windshield, forward seating, individual console seats, and rear jump seats. Seating is safe and secure for the youngest (or oldest) of mariners. The design provides ample cockpit space for fishing. These boats generally come fish-ready, with fish storage boxes either on the deck centerline or forward under the bow seats, a live baitwell, and fishing rod holders. They are almost always self-bailing and most feature a fiberglass deck for easy cleanup.

A dual console boat will not ride as dry as a center console or walk-around cuddy, but it is an excellent choice for lakes and rivers. When the weather turns bad, you can close the windshield and duck under the top for a good

Dual console. (Photograph of 202 Sportsman courtesy of Pro-Line Boats)

measure of protection. Dual consoles are almost always under 22 feet and are usually easy to trailer and handle.

Dual consoles are an excellent choice for watersports. In a well-thought-out design, a centerline fish box will double as a ski locker (but watch that smell). The interior lends itself to secure seating as well as easy ingress and egress. A top choice for a family boat and a good day-fishing boat, the dual console is almost always a modified V. But for the few boats over 22 feet, a deep V may be preferable.

5. Bass Boat

These smaller fishing rigs are used almost exclusively in lakes and back river country for freshwater fishing. They run from 14 feet to around 21 feet. Most bass boaters prefer to get to their favorite fishing holes quickly, so they usually carry the upper limit in outboard power. Bass boats are usually a modified V hull.

Bass boats have seating for three or four adults but are usually fished by just two. A typical model will feature

Bass boat. (*Photograph of 205 Pro DC courtesy of ProCraft Boats*)

treated wood or aluminum decks topped with carpeting, a live baitwell, and a larger fish storage box. A trolling motor on the bow rounds this rig off nicely.

Bass boats are not usually self-bailing, so water taken on must be pumped overboard. Most bass boaters wouldn't be caught dead carrying a bimini or convertible top, so if the weather turns, you either out-run the rain or get wet. With all that speed, most bass boats are great for watersports. Safe seating is usually limited to two or three persons, so this is not the boat for a family outing.

6. Bowrider

A bowrider is a great family day boat powered by an out-board or inboard/outboard, generally for river or lake use. A bowrider is usually carpeted, so it's not ideal for fishing; but it beats fishing off the bridge. The design al-lows for plenty of secure seating: children love it up front even though it usually gets a little wet up there. Adorned with bolster cushions, sunpads, bench seats, and cuphold-ers, these are built for comfort and speed. Upkeep and cleanup are a little more involved. But a little luxury is usually worth it, isn't it?

There are two distinct types of bowriders as far as I'm concerned. The fully carpeted type has a treated wood deck below the carpet. I refer to these as rug boats. Then there are the bowriders with a gelcoated fiberglass deck with snap-in carpet. The former is considerably less expensive and, when maintained and stored correctly, will give you many years of great service. The fiberglass deck is preferable: it's easier to clean, better built (no exposed wood to go bad), and longer lasting. It's also more expensive.

These boats are not, as a rule, self-bailing, so any water taken on drains into the bilge and must be pumped overboard. Keep this in mind if you're storing in a wet slip. Frequent rains mean a frequent drain on the batteries that power the automatic bilge pump. Keep a battery charger or spare battery close at hand. If you're storing this boat on a trailer, pull the plug and allow rain to run out of the bilge on its own.

Weather protection is much the same as on a dual console. On a bowrider, however, folks usually get

Many manufacturers use the same hull for small cuddies (left), and bowriders (right), as seen here with Chaparral's 2135 small cuddy and 2130 Sport bowrider. (Courtesy of Chaparral)

a little more involved in canvas. You will often see wrap-around canvas (weather protection) or even camper canvas (with stand-up headroom, screens, and total coverage). If the boat is stored outdoors, a mooring or storage cover is a must to protect all those vinyl cushions and carpets.

Bowriders usually offer a lot of storage, even space for water skis. Larger, newer models may feature an enclosed head. I tend to favor a modified V here, particularly for the smaller ones. But I've tested some nice larger, deep V configurations.

7. Small Cuddy

The deck layout of a small cuddy boat is similar to that of the bowrider. In fact, many manufacturers use the same hull for bowriders and cuddies and modify only the interior. The main difference is that the cuddy has no forward seating; instead, there is a small cabin with limited headroom. Providing shelter from the weather and usually a portable marine head below, these boats are great for young families.

Seating in a cuddy design is limited but secure. They have the same flooring types as a bowrider and are generally not self-bailing. It's worth noting that to anchor or dock, you have to walk on the slanted top of the cabin; this is sometimes a little tricky. Small cuddies are powered by outboards, which allow more cockpit space, or inboard/outboards, which offer better fuel efficiency.

With the cabin forward, cuddy designs tend to give a drier ride than similar-sized bowriders. They are also great for watersports, as long as you have a small crew. A small cuddy under 21 feet should not be taken offshore. Most manufacturers offer a modified V hull in these sizes.

8. Larger Cruiser

Larger cruiser. (Photograph of 300 Signature courtesy of Chaparral)

Starting at around 23 feet, these cabin boats are great for overnights and weekending. Nicely appointed for the whole family, they usually have stand-up headroom below, a galley, an enclosed head (some with a shower), and sleeping accommodations for at least two and usually four. Seating may be limited in the smaller ones, but it's usually secure. Larger cruisers have all of the deck amenities, from bench seats to lounges to sunpads.

Larger cruisers can operate in sheltered waters or offshore. As with any larger, heavier boat, these cruisers tend to draw more. Larger cruisers almost always have a deep V hull design. If you boat in shallower areas, this is a very real concern and should be addressed before you make your purchase.

Larger cruisers offer excellent weather protection. The larger, deeper hull design does not lend itself well to watersports. They are usually self-bailing (make sure you check) with fiberglass flooring and snap-in carpet. As with the larger cruiser's cousin, the smaller cuddy, you must walk through the windshield and onto a slanted foredeck to anchor or dock. Larger models may feature dockside air conditioning (110 volt), and 27- or 28-footers may even have room for a water-cooled generator that allows you to run the air-conditioning while out on the water. All the comforts of home!

I should mention here the advantages and disadvantages of two motors, or twin screws. There is a great deal of debate over when two motors are necessary and whether they are outboards, inboard/outboards, or inboards. Modern engines are infinitely more reliable than earlier models. Unless you frequently head well offshore, carrying a radio is far better than paying for the upkeep, repair, and fuel of a second motor. You can become a member of Seatow for around $100 per year (rates vary), and they'll come and get you anytime you have a motor problem. If you must, carry a smaller portable outboard and tank (known as a kicker) that can be attached to the stern to get you home in emergencies. A twin-motor boat will generally only travel at hull speed (7 to 10 knots) on one of its main engines. A kicker will accomplish the same for far less money. Upkeep is far less; however, regular maintenance and start-ups of the kicker are recommended.

The matter of maneuverability and top speed is another question altogether. Even a 24-foot cruiser can be a handful to dock in strong winds and currents. Twin motors allow you to use the forward and reverse gears to steer the boat, and they greatly increase your maneuverability, particularly in tight spaces. I definitely recommend twin screws on boats 28 feet long or larger, but—as stated earlier—they can be quite useful on a 24-footer.

TIP

Go for twin engines when long offshore trips and better handling are priorities.

As for performance, the more motor, the more power.

9. Deckboat

Deckboat. (Photograph of 233 Sunesta courtesy of Chaparral)

Not a new idea but swiftly gaining in popularity, the deckboat is great for large families or groups. These boats look a lot like pontoon boats, but don't be fooled: deckboats can move. With a flatter, modified V hull design, they generally plane quickly and are very stable.

Even the smaller deckboats provide secure seating for at least eight people, and with ample deck amenities—lounges, sunpads, cupholders—they are great boats for entertaining. Roomy, open, fairly fast, and able to be used for watersports, day trips, or touring, deckboats are probably best suited to rivers and lakes. Larger models may have a separate room for the portable marine head. As a rule they offer tons of storage.

Most newer models feature fiberglass decks that are self-bailing and easily set up for fishing. A typical deckboat will have relatively low gunwales and give a wetter ride than the boat types discussed above. Deckboats offer poor weather protection unless they're outfitted with a cumbersome canvas enclosure, though, like bowriders, many carry a great amount of stuff. They may be powered by outboard or inboard/outboard motors.

10. Pontoon Boat

Pontoon boat. (Photograph of 824 Elite courtesy of Sylvan Marine)

These are roomy, basic platform boats usually powered by smaller outboards. Most aluminum pontoon boats cannot get up on a plane, so they're pretty slow. However, the catamaran hull design allows for a smaller motor and great maneuverability.

Although they are used quite a bit in salt water, pontoon boats are primarily lake and river boats. Wiring is usually run exposed under the plywood deck and is prone to corrosion in the saltwater environment. The outboard motors tend to ride low, close to the water, and may become immersed when running in a choppy bay. Freshwater immersion is bad, but immersion in salt water can be catastrophic.

Pontoon boats offer lots of secure seating. They are easy to operate in lakes and rivers and very stable. The decks are generally carpeting over marine plywood. Like deckboats, they offer poor weather protection without a canvas awning. Some feature a pop-up changing room, which houses the portable marine head.

If you plan to take aluminum pontoons into salt water, you must be certain that they have been treated (a process called *etching*). Pontoon tubes, side walls, and grab rails are all at risk of pitting. Call the manufacturer with the hull serial number and ask if the aluminum has been treated. Or better yet, keep the boat in a lake.

11. Jet Boat

Jet boat. (Photograph courtesy of Bombardier Recreational Products)

Jet boats have recently enjoyed a brief flare-up of popularity. They are generally very small, fast, and wet. Sizes range from 12 to 18 feet, with very flat hull configurations, which makes them great for shallow-water applications. Most offer a modified V at best. The nicer ones feature a center console, but most have a side console and tend to list when you're onboard alone.

Jet boats are run by an outboard powerhead mounted inside the stern engine compartment, with a jet drive propulsion unit mounted through the transom. Unless heavily insulated and properly mounted, they tend to be noisy and vibrate the boat at lower and higher speeds. Directional control is accomplished through the jetted water, and the boats lose maneuverability at idle speeds, such as when docking. You must head in the desired direction and "bump" the throttle to gain steerage.

Jet boats can be very fun at high speeds, but they are good for watersports and little else. Single engine models are not quick "out of the hole." And while they can pull a tube or a kneeboard, they are not good for skiing. Some may have a bimini top option and perhaps a storage cover. Seating for four is common, although some larger models can seat six.

In an effort to increase their popularity, there are some newer models offered with twin engines, which increase speed and maneuverability, and they can even tow a skier. They're fun but are limited in their versatility.

12. Personal Watercraft (PWC), or Jet Ski

Personal watercraft (PWC) or jet ski. (Photograph courtesy of Bombardier Recreational Products)

We have all seen jet skis: a sort of waterborne motorcycle that can carry up to three people. A jet ski is great fun—

virtually a watersport in itself. Jet skis are wet but can be dangerous if mishandled.

There are two basic types. The ski type is ridden standing up and maneuvered mostly through balance. It is difficult to "get up on" when taking off, and is not very popular except in competition races. The waverunner type is operated while the rider is seated, much like a snowmobile or motorcycle, and maneuvered through a combination of steering and balance. It is easier for the novice to balance and ride.

You're required to wear a ski-type life vest at all times while operating a jet ski, as the possibility of falling off is ever present. Newer models are extremely fast and should be handled respectfully. The newer models also carry more fuel than earlier models, usually enough for a full day out.

13. Performance/Ski Boat

Performance/ski boat. (Photograph of 22 ZX courtesy of Donzi)

These boats have one purpose: pure speed. The smaller ones are great for watersports, whereas the larger ones are

great for salt- or freshwater racing (sanctioned, please!).
They come in a range of configurations, from small four-
seaters to much larger, cuddy-cabin types.

The smaller performance/ski boats have modified
V hulls, huge outboard motors, and low freeboard (the
height between the waterline and the deck). Their single
function is to plane quickly and tow skiers. They are great
on the lakes and rivers, but they offer a wet and dangerous ride in rough water.

For serious skiing, however, it's hard to beat the
single-inboard models favored in the Northeast. These
also plane quickly and create a better wake or wave pattern for competition skiing. These boats usually have
higher freeboard and nicer seating than their smaller outboard cousins.

Another option is the small performance-hull
type. It is driven with an inboard/outboard engine
and is also very fast. Comfortable but limited seating
takes up all of the small cockpit area. Usually a sun-
pad will cover the engine compartment, and the bow
will be closed. Fast, loud, and sexy are the major
criteria here.

The larger toys (21 feet and above) are deep V
and are great for offshore use. Getting out and going
fast in rough water is what they do best. They are generally not self-bailing because the unusually deep V
puts the deck area below the waterline. Most performance boatowners feel that the louder and faster your
boat is, the better. Performance boats are great fun
even if a little dangerous. Larger models feature enclosed heads, full galleys, and sleeping for four. They
generally offer very little headroom. They always offer
lots of power. These are almost exclusively inboard/
outboards and come in single and twin configurations,
depending on your need for speed.

14. Catamaran Hulls

Catamaran hull. (Photograph of Talon T-22 courtesy of Talon Marine)

Catamaran hulls are versatile and usually fast. They have unique handling characteristics and—when operated well—are recognized as some of the best riding boats out there. From center console, to walk-around cuddy, to deckboat, to racing hulls: they can do it all. Usually self-bailing, most require two motors and are pricey. The twin hull design usually provides for expansive deck space.

There are of course other types of boats—aluminum jon boats, canoes, and inflatables, not to mention nonplaning powerboats. I choose to limit our discussion to the above 14 types because they are the most common under 30 feet. With a little imagination, however, this guide can apply to any boat.

What Are Your Boat Needs? A Questionnaire

The following questions contain the criteria you should consider when purchasing a boat. Please take a minute and review them to save yourself time and money.

1. How many people will you routinely carry aboard? This not only helps to determine the size of the vessel, but also helps with seating configuration, safety considerations, and use priority. A crew of four may enjoy the day out on a 17-foot runabout, but six people would be cramped. Here are some loose guidelines (see also Capacity Plates, page 35). If the boat will normally carry

▫ **two to four people**, you'll want a 15- to 17-foot boat

▫ **four to six people**, you'll want a 19- to 21-foot boat

▫ **six to eight people**, you'll want a 23- to 25-foot boat

▫ **eight or more people**, you'll want a boat of at least 26 feet, although you can get away with something a bit smaller in a deck or pontoon boat

2. Do you plan to carry young children?
Safety is the biggest question here. The depth of the cockpit is one major concern. A deep cockpit makes a safe playpen. Secure seating, shade, and cabin or facilities for a head are a few more concerns.

3. What is your main interest in being out on the water (choose at least one)? This is quite possibly the most important question of all. If you feel tempted to circle more than three items, stop and reconsider your main interests by asking yourself the question: What would I be doing on my ideal boating day?

For example, if your priority is fishing and diving on the ocean, this would dictate a center console or walk-around cuddy of at least 19 feet. A boat for recreation, water skiing, and taking day trips for a small family may call for a bowrider, a dual console, or a center console as small as 17 feet, or a

TIP

If you plan on having small children aboard, look for a deep, protective cockpit, secure seating, shelter from the elements, and a portable marine head.

General Purpose	Specific Purpose	Boat Types
Family	recreation, day trips, touring	1, 3, 4, 6, 7, 8, 9, 10, 14
Fishing	ocean, river, flats, diving	1, 2, 3, 4, 5, 13, 14
Cruising	day trips, overnighting, weekending	6, 7, 8, 13
Watersports	skiing, kneeboarding, tubing	any types except 2 or 10
Speed	racing, day trip, range/time	5, 6, 7, 13, 14
Business	capacity, range, function	1, 3, 5, 8, 9, 10, 13, 14

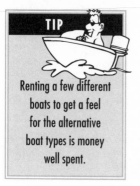

TIP

Renting a few different boats to get a feel for the alternative boat types is money well spent.

small cuddy of at least 19 feet. A larger family or passenger list dictates more seating, and the size should increase. Remember that a center console has room but lacks seating. Try to use your best judgment; these are only guidelines and suggestions.

If you're purchasing an inexpensive boat with the idea of upgrading next year, you obviously have more latitude than if you're financing a newer boat for 5 to 10 years. What you should try to avoid is being in a position where a year or two down the road, you're unhappy with your choice and must sell at a loss to get the boat you should have purchased in the first place.

If you truly can't decide, rent a few different types of boats or go out with friends. Try to experience the handling characteristics of a couple different types of boats. It's better to spend a few hundred dollars here than to suffer for years with the wrong choice.

4. How many years or months of boating experience do you have? Although you want to avoid purchasing less boat than you'll need three years from now, the opposite goes for inexperienced boaters purchasing larger, more impressive boats that are hard to

Capacity Plates

Since 1972 the Coast Guard has required manufacturers of monohull boats under 20 feet in length to display loading and capacity information on the finished vessel. This refers to the maximum weight of people in pounds that can be safely carried, as well as the maximum combined weight of people, fuel, and gear that can be carried.

Sailboats, canoes, kayaks, and inflatables are exempt from this requirement. Boats powered by outboard motors are also required to display maximum horsepower capacity; boats powered by inboard or inboard/outboard motors are not. Since 1980 builders have also been required to display the maximum number of people a boat can accommodate, in addition to their weight.

All this information appears on *capacity labels* or *plates*, which should be mounted in plain view of one boarding or operating the boat. Some builders display the capacity rating in combination with other information, such as when and where the boat was built or its compliance with other standards. Many builders voluntarily provide capacity information on boats not covered by the rule, such as inflatables and boats over 20 feet. Bear in mind that capacity limits are determined for good to moderate conditions. Do not load the boat to capacity under adverse conditions. If you can't find capacity information displayed on a boat, the best course of action is to contact the manufacturer.

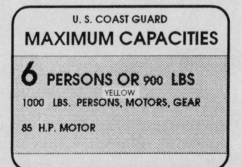

A standard form in which capacity information is displayed on vessels.

(Boating Safety Circular 64, *U.S. Department of Transportation, United States Coast Guard, Dec. 1996*)

handle singlehanded. Again, a good idea may be to rent a larger boat in the configuration you have chosen to get a feel for the handling characteristics. For newer boaters, many areas have a local chapter of the U.S. Power Squadrons, which will offer inexpensive yet very thorough basic seamanship courses. I heartily recommend such courses to all.

5. How is your mechanical aptitude in minor electrical repairs and minor engine repairs? This is a huge consideration for the used-boat buyer. It's virtually impossible to find every possible flaw or defect in a two- or three-year-old boat, and this problem multiplies with the boat's age. You should be able to do some basic wiring and testing (salt air corrodes connections) and have a working knowledge of your motor and fuel system. Do you have a basic tool kit to carry aboard? Boat maintenance is not as complicated as it seems, and the basics are covered in the boat inspection and maintenance sections of this book.

However, if electrical and mechanical work is truly not your forte, you might be well advised to head over to the new boat department. The money you hoped to save by buying used may—and in practice usually will—end up in your mechanic's vacation fund.

TRAP

Can you handle minor electrical repairs and routine engine maintenance? If not, seriously consider a new boat.

6. What is your estimated total budget? Your total monthly payment? A salesperson, like a car salesman, will always try to get you into the biggest boat you can afford (or perhaps would rather not afford). Set a firm monthly budget for yourself, which should also include insurance costs ($50 or more per month), storage, maintenance (better allow at least $25 per month), and fuel and supplies. In appendix 1 we will cover what is involved in financing and how to negotiate the best rate and terms. We also cover boat insurance briefly.

7. What is your time frame for purchase? It's good to get a feel for market conditions; but a given used boat may not be available next week, let alone next month. And a new-boat price may be good only for that particular vessel (not one that is ordered in) and may not be good for more than two or three weeks. Keep in mind that the ability to buy *today* is a powerful bargaining tool. The best new-boat deals can be had at the end of the model year (May, June, and July), just as with cars.

8. How often will you really use the boat? I can't count how many times someone has purchased a beautiful new boat for over $20,000 and could not find the time to use it. That is a lot of money to leave tied up at the dock. Better to buy a less expensive, used boat.

9. Will there be a partner involved? You can often buy more boat with a partner. But like all partnerships, this is a little risky. Issues such as fueling, the cost of maintenance and repair, and even designated use days need to be addressed. In addition, some insurance companies consider two unrelated persons signed on a title as a business partnership or even uninsurable. Be sure to check before the purchase.

One Hand for the Boat

A very experienced boater (by his own account) came through the marina the other day telling stories of how he often takes his 18-foot center console from Florida to the Bahamas by himself. Minutes after he pulled away, we noticed his center console running at speed in tight circles out on the bay, with no one at the controls. He had carelessly fallen overboard. (He later said that he had to dive three times to avoid the boat and the prop.) Eventually he was saved by some rather brave jet skiers. Oh, the shame.

10. Who will be the primary users? Piloting a boat is a tremendous responsibility—similar to driving a car but with several major differences. Virtually no one needs a driver's license. There are no lines on the road, the road moves, and half the time you're not sure where the road is! Be sure that the person who uses your boat is knowledgeable and responsible. Again, I strongly recommend that you insist on a Power Squadrons course for all of your regular users. As the owner, you may be liable in the event of an accident, regardless of who was at the helm.

11. How will you handle maintenance and cleaning responsibilities? Your boat will require consistent maintenance to retain its optimum resale value.

12. Will you be trailering the boat? If so, what type of vehicle will you be using? Where will you be storing the boat? These are all major considerations in your purchase. If you plan on trailering, you need to know the towing capacity of your vehicle. If in doubt, contact a dealership that sells your make of vehicle. With a little patience you can determine the towing capacity of any vehicle, regardless of age. Do not exceed the manufacturer's suggested towing capacity. If you do, you're jeopardizing the engine, transmission, and suspension of your vehicle—not to mention the safety of your passengers, yourself, and anyone sharing the road with you.

In Florida, any new trailer with a 3,000-pound capacity must have brakes. Even if your state does not have a similar requirement, it's a good one to adopt.

If you plan to keep the boat in salt water, an inboard/outboard is a poor choice because the salt water will corrode the lower unit and cause you a lot of problems. In this case outboards are preferable. In a freshwater environment, this is less of a concern.

If you must rent storage, how much will it cost? When will your boat be available for use? Is it in a secure area?

When storing a boat at a wet slip, it's preferable to have a self-bailing hull. If not, you should have an automatic bilge pump float switch to remove rainwater. Be sure to keep your battery charged or constant use of the bilge pump will drain the battery and the pump will no longer work. A good insurance policy will be needed shortly thereafter. In addition, try to dock with the bow towards any significant wave action.

13. Where will you be using the boat? A saltwater environment is much harsher than freshwater. The saltwater environment will corrode metal almost from the start. You must purchase the correct boat for these conditions and maintain your boat and motor accordingly. Boating on the ocean or on any large, open body of water raises a host of questions about seaworthiness. These should inform your choices.

These questions should help you to determine your priorities, wants, and needs. Once you have a clear idea of the type of boat you want, you may begin to shop brands, pricing, and options.

Docking Tips

A friend of mine purchased a speedboat—a low-profile catamaran hull, motor, and trailer—at a great price. Three weeks later, after an afternoon of fun on the water, he decided to leave it at a neighbor's dock overnight. (Given what follows, I want to assure you that I wasn't there that day.) He tied the boat up with its stern facing out on a large, open bay on a river. The top of the transom was only inches above the waterline to begin with, and the larger wave action of the bay swamped and sank the boat in 4 feet of water. We saved the boat and motor, but it has electrical problems to this day. Always dock with the bow facing any significant wave action. If you have limited experience on the water, sign up for a basic seamanship course such as those offered by the U.S. Power Squadrons.

Buying a Used Boat

PART 2

Let's face it: the main purpose of buying a used boat is to save money. If money were not a factor, most of us would rather buy new. I have personally purchased hundreds of used boats and done quite well. My purpose was resale, so the objectives I set for myself were a bit more stringent than those before us now. Our goal here is to purchase a boat at a bargain price with the idea of breaking even or perhaps making a modest profit a year or two down the road when it's time to upgrade. The average boat loses around 10 percent of its value per year. Add in maintenance and repair and you'll find your target area.

The whole process of used-boat shopping can be time consuming, but it should also be fun. The system I use will cut down tremendously on the actual time you'll spend going out and looking. Most of my shopping is done from my favorite chair at home. This sure beats driving 50 miles one way to see a misrepresented piece of junk. They say that one person's trash is another's treasure. Don't go there! It's much more fun to weed out the prospects over the phone and then spend a day looking at some really fine vessels.

Avoid setting unrealistic limits on money and time. All too often, I have impatiently tied up my available capital—only to find the best deal right around the corner, yet now out of reach. Choose your boat and your target budget carefully. There is a tremendous

temptation to buy more than you really want to afford.
Be patient: your boat is out there. It just may not go on
sale until next week.

Dealing with an individual rather than a dealership poses its own set of challenges. Believe me, the ag-
gravation is worth it. I have bought and sold hundreds of
boats from individuals and made a great deal of money.
I'm proud to say that the worst I've done is to break
even twice. First, let's establish some ground rules. We'll
go into greater detail as we go.

Here are the ten commandments of used-boat
shopping.

1. Never buy someone else's junk, regardless of the
    price.
2. If it looks bad at first glance, it probably is.
3. If it seems too good to be true, it probably is.
4. If they haven't taken care of the minor details, they
    probably haven't taken care of the major ones.
5. If it's dirty now, it has probably always been dirty.
6. If you think the seller isn't being totally forth-
    coming, he's probably not.
7. If you see several rough homemade repairs, run
    away!
8. Always do a mechanical inspection or have one
    done by a certified technician.
9. Always take the boat for a sea trial.
10. Money talks. Bring some.

The moral of the story is this: you're not necessarily looking for that one-in-a-thousand killer deal.
What you're looking to do is take an acceptable deal and
turn it into an excellent deal with a proper greeting, a
thorough inspection, a little pricing information, the
ability—if not necessarily the willingness—to buy today,
and some negotiation. I generally only make one offer
and, if I want the boat badly enough, may increase my
bid marginally. I try to avoid a haggling situation. It's

better to leave your phone number and walk away. At that point, whoever calls back first loses (more on that thought later).

Your first impression is probably correct. I've gotten pretty far trusting my instincts. You're fooling yourself to believe that a bargain fixer-upper will be a good deal. Chances are that if the present owner hasn't paid to fix smaller problems, the larger, really expensive ones may be just around the corner. Obvious neglect is a sure sign of a general lack of maintenance. Avoid these boats.

I'm assuming that you're starting out as I did: inexperienced in boating and all that it involves. If you have a lot of experience or a background in marine mechanics and wiring, feel free to bend the rules a little. I had a little wholesale business going where I would buy less desirable boats and have my partner fix them up. We'd then sell the repaired boats and split the profits.

Having said that, there are a lot of well maintained, beautiful used boats out there to be had at bargain prices—if only you know how and where to look. Let's go get them!

5 Shopping by Phone: Individual Ads

Local classified ads often contain excellent prospects. After these, I'd try *Boat Trader* and similar publications that feature individual ads with pictures, descriptions, and pricing. When I first started, I used a publication with pictures to identify different models but made most of my deals through the classifieds. This is a great way to begin and will save you lots of time and money. Also stop and check out boats on the roadside with for sale signs on them, if you have the time, or make a note of the location and return. The advantage here is that you can

TIP

Save time and hassle: shop by phone before you shop by car.

make a brief inspection on your own and then, if you like what you see, make the call.

Keep a legal pad handy and take detailed notes. I like to cut out the ad and tape it to the page. Hopefully by this point you've established your budget and a target group of boats. Call and inquire about any boat in your target group that doesn't exceed your budget range by more than 25 to 35 percent. Be prepared. A few minutes with some well-thought-out questions now can save you a lot of fruitless trips out to the boonies. Here are some good questions to ask at this point.

🔲 **Have you had any major repair work done since you've owned the boat?** Older outboards will hopefully have been rebuilt. It should be noted here that most marine mechanics agree that a motor run continuously for 11 or 12 years in salt water is not worth rebuilding, whether or not it has been flushed regularly. The inside water jackets (and any other parts in continuous contact with the salt water) may well be corroded beyond repair. If you wish to buy a boat with such an outboard, be sure that you're buying the entire package for hull value only. Set aside enough money for repowering and installation.

🔲 **Who did the repairs?** Hopefully a reputable marine yard and not Cousin Vinnie.

🔲 **Are the vinyl seats or bolsters cracked or split? What is the condition of the canvas top?** Be specific here: vinyl and canvas costs are way up there.

🔲 **Is the deck the original or has it been replaced?** Replaced flooring may indicate serious problems below—or simply a poorly built boat. The question is unnecessary with newer boats.

▣ **Has the boat been stored in the water?** Once a boat has been kept in salt water, it's practically impossible to restore the gelcoat below the waterline to its original state: the effects of sanding, scraping, and bottom painting are irreversible. You will most likely continue painting the bottom, which is an annual maintenance chore that is costly and time-consuming. An inboard/outboard stored in salt water may also have serious problems as a result. The same goes for outboards if the lower unit or bracket was immersed for long periods.

▣ **How's the steering? Does the boat turn easily end to end?**

▣ **Does the tilt/trim work properly? Are there any hydraulic fluid leaks?**

▣ **How well does the motor run?**

▣ **Do all the electrical systems and gauges work?**

▣ **Last but not least: are you flexible on price?** At this point, you don't really care: you haven't even seen the boat, but you just want to plant the seed.

It should go without saying that you should ask about options, trailer, canvas, and electronics. Make detailed notes next to the taped-on ad. Note the location and get directions. Some of these boats will be hot items worth seeing at the first opportune moment. First come, first served always applies here.

There is certainly no lack of questions to ask. Don't get too specific or negative at this point. Hesitation and excuses on the seller's part ("It's an old boat, so of course some things don't work") can be an indication of bigger problems not discussed. If they appear to be hiding something, you'll have to decide if it's still a good enough deal to warrant a visit. This can be a

TIP

An asking price is just that. When shopping the classifieds, consider boats priced up to 35 percent above your target price.

tough call. If you can't make up your mind, go anyway. People hesitate to talk for different reasons, not all of them bad. I've pursued a number of boats this way and have been handsomely rewarded. If there are more promising boat deals out there, go after those first and put the questionable ones in reserve.

We'll handle the other, more important questions face to face. At this point, we are only trying to determine overall condition, if the boat suits your wants and needs, and if it's worth seeing and when.

6 Shopping by Phone: Dealerships

I should tell you now that this avenue would be my second choice. A dealership does offer some advantages. They ideally will have checked out the boat and can vouch for its reliability, and you will develop a relationship with someone in the business who will be attentive to your wants and needs. But these benefits need to have some monetary value to you. I say monetary value because you generally will not find the best deals here. The dealership does this for a living, every day of the year. Whatever savings you may hope to gain by buying under market value have usually been taken up by the dealership to cover commissions, overhead, etc. They're the professionals; we're the amateurs.

That said, the dealerships are worth a look. In general you have a better chance of getting a good deal on a consignment boat than on a trade-in. With a consignment boat, the salesperson is working on commis-

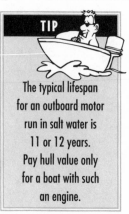

TIP

The typical lifespan for an outboard motor run in salt water is 11 or 12 years. Pay hull value only for a boat with such an engine.

sion as an intermediary between you and the owner; with a trade-in, the dealership already has a substantial investment in the boat. You can still find good deals at slightly under market value. Remember that a boat dealership almost always gets a better price for their used boats than an individual owner would. You may easily assume around 10 percent more.

A visit to a dealership can also be a crash course in market values and available models and manufacturers. You'll hear from the horse's mouth which manufacturers are good, bad, or ugly (albeit with some small prejudice toward their inventory). You'll be able to view a greater number of boats in a shorter period of time with less effort. You can ask bolder questions, pick up on some insight from your salesperson, and possibly find a friend in the business.

Your initial call should be similar to the one outlined in the previous section on dealing with individuals. You can get more specific about condition, price flexibility, maintenance history, and the like because the salesperson represents the product: he doesn't own it. He won't have the emotional attachment, nor should he

TIP

When shopping a used-boat dealership you'll get your best deal on a consignment boat.

feel slighted when presented with some specific questions and concerns. See if you can befriend him by keeping it light and friendly. Ask the salesperson for his personal opinion. For example: Would you buy this boat for yourself? Would you buy it for your family? When I sold for dealerships, I would always express my true opinion when asked.

If the salesperson sounds like a fast talker, he probably is. If he sounds sincere, give him a shot. Ask a few direct questions.

▣ How long has the boat been for sale on the lot?

▣ Is it a consignment boat or trade-in?

▣ Has the marina done a mechanical inspection? What were the results?

▣ Is there any transferable warranty? Does it cost anything to transfer?

▣ Has the salesperson had the boat out on the water?

▣ Does anyone there know the history of the boat? Are there any maintenance records?

▣ Is there any flexibility on price?

▣ What is the N.A.D.A. or ABOS Book (commonly called the Blue Book) value on the boat? (See the following section on pricing for more information.)

The more he knows, the better I feel. If he seems to be guessing, give him a list of questions and have him call you back. Yes, go ahead and give him your number. He'll be much more cooperative and helpful if you let him know you're interested enough to allow him to have some of your personal information. Do not let him interview you. It isn't necessary for him to know your boating preferences, family situation, credit status, etc. A good way to prevent this is to ask him if there are any other similar boats on his lot for sale. Ask him to have some suggestions ready when he calls you back.

It's the salesperson's job to control the course of the sale. You shouldn't begrudge a person for trying to do his job. However, he needn't be in control to work with you. If he begins to be overbearing, back off and begin to terminate the conversation. If he's sincerely trying to work with you, he'll back down immediately rather than lose you. Remember that the ability to walk away from a deal can save you thousands of dollars.

Let him know you're interested (if you are) and tell him you'll come by in a couple of days. There is no need to make an appointment. Get his name and write it down. Promise to look for him when you arrive, and then do so. It's better to cultivate a friend in the business than to deal with someone who is just out to get your money. Additionally, he may be of help in the future if you maintain a friendly relationship (see the following section).

Pricing

How do you know what a used boat is worth? I personally went through a lot of trial and error in this area when I first started, but I was rewarded well for my efforts. The key here is to analyze the market and take notes. I did a lot of market analysis on my own, mainly through the newspaper classifieds and the trader magazines. I wasn't online until much later. I never lost money on a boat that I'd purchased for resale.

Let's start with the trader-type magazines. They will show you pictures and give descriptions and pricing. Take all of this with a grain of salt. Asking price is rarely the take price, and it may vary from 10 percent to as much as 30 percent or more! I would look at any given ad and assume that the intended take price is 5 to 10 percent less than posted, and your actual target value is 15 to 20 percent less for a boat in better than average condition.

If you doubt this, make a few investigative calls and feel the seller out for an immediate 10 percent price re-

TIP

Don't take the prices in the classifieds and trader-type magazines at face value.

duction for cash. I can assure you that very few will turn you down outright. Try to be as polite about this as possible: an insulted seller probably won't take 100 percent of the asking price! If you're polite, most won't commit but will indicate some flexibility and invite you down for a look. When you're dealing in person and using my approach, you can usually get a seller to come down another 5 percent. On a $10,000 boat, you've just saved $1,500.

Don't try to discuss price seriously over the phone for a boat you actually wish to purchase. This example is merely for market research, not shopping.

There is an alternative method. Every marina has a "Blue Book" or reference book that gives the national average wholesale and retail value of used boats and motors. Nearly all of the boat manufacturers are represented here. Since these are impartial service publications and unbiased in their estimates, they provide an excellent source for pricing information.

There are three commonly used reference books: the ABOS book (Blue Book), the *N.A.D.A. Appraisal Guide*, and the *BUC Used Boat Price Book*. I've listed them in order of preference, but they're all good. A determined consumer could get his or her hands on a copy of these guides; but they are typically intended for use within the industry and their prices are prohibitive for the average consumer. (The last time I checked, the BUC books covering boats built between 1981 and 1998 went for around $150; the N.A.D.A. publication covering the same time range could be had for around $100 as part of a one-year subscription arrangement.) N.A.D.A. publishes a consumer version of its

TRAP

Don't try to discuss pricing seriously over the phone.

appraisal guide at a more manageable price (around $35), although it's not as comprehensive as the dealer's copy.

My first suggestion is to cultivate a relationship with a person in the business to get access to a dealer's Blue Book. This is not as difficult as it seems. If you've been out there shopping at marinas and boat dealers and consignment lots, you may have already met your contact. That nice salesperson with the laid-back attitude you got along with so well is the perfect candidate. Let him know that you like his marina and intend to have your service work done there—and mean it. If he takes the long view of his job, he'll help you. Next year, you may be looking for that new boat he's shown you. If you cannot be sincere about this, choose someone with whom you can be. Do not overuse this connection.

Only one boat per call, and no more than two calls per week. You may think this is an elaborate route to getting a price quote (as we see in the next section on the Internet, N.A.D.A. information is now available online). But pricing information is only part of our purpose. I can't overstate the value of having a friend in the business who understands the local market in which you will most likely buy your boat. You can often just call a marina unannounced, ask for a price reference, and get favorable results. But don't be offended if you get a flat-out refusal of cooperation. These price books are considered privileged information by some, and those individuals are reluctant to give up that information without hope of selling you one of their boats. You may want to ask what they have available for sale at their yard first and establish a little rapport. Who knows—they may have just what you're looking for!

Marine lenders also use these guides, so your bank loan officer may also be able to help with price information. If so, you shouldn't count on using this service more than a few times so be fairly focused in your interest be-

TIP

Decide how much you'd pay for a boat before you see it.

fore calling. Again, only ask about one boat per call.

As valuable as they are, these marine pricing guides should be seen as another resource and not the final word. Because they average national sales data, these guides may not accurately reflect the value of a boat in your area. I've found that the prices in the classified ads tend to be more accurate and reflect local market conditions better, and overall, I've found the best deals here. When you feel comfortable with your target area and pricing, follow these ads daily. I've gotten some of my best deals being the first to arrive with a cash offer.

Once you have established that a boat is worth seeing, decide how much you wish to pay for it before leaving the house. Write it down in your notes. This is very important, as you'll learn in the negotiation section.

The Internet

I touched briefly on the Internet in section 1, but I'll elaborate here.

If you're hooked up and reasonably good at searching, this one tool can save you a lot of time, effort, and money. I'll give you my two best sources here. The first is Trader Online at <http://www.traderonline.com/>. Once you get to the homepage, go to the boat trader section and bookmark it. Assuming you have narrowed down your search to a handful of boats, you can search the nationwide boat database according to manufacturer. I limit my search to my telephone area code (you can search up to three area codes at once). Use as many of the available criteria as you like to customize your search.

I've always had the best results with Trader Online, but Soundings Marine Datanet <*http:// www.soundingspub.com/*> and All About Boats <*http://www.allaboutboats.com/*> both offer large databases of used boats for sale and are worth a look. About.com's pages on Powerboating <*http://www. powerboat.about.com/*> also provide dozens of links to used-boat sites.

With a little perseverance you can access the classified sections of all of the local newspapers in your target area. Most popular browsers provide links to newspapers. Once you reach the site for a paper, follow the instructions and get to the classifieds. Many classified sections will allow you to search for new ads posted that very day. They are usually updated by seven o'clock in the morning so you can check them out bright and early while sipping on your first cup of coffee. I wish I'd had that luxury when I started.

My other favorite site—and I hate to part with this one—is the N.A.D.A. Appraisal Guide site <*http://www.nadaguides.com/*>, where pricing information from the well-known N.A.D.A. guide discussed in the previous section is posted online. Like the consumer version of the N.A.D.A guide, the website is not as thorough as the dealer's copy; but it's nonetheless a great resource. When you get to the homepage, hit the pricing key (Get Values On-Line) and follow the instructions to get to your target boat or boats. The instructions show the alphabet; click on the letter that your boat manufacturer's name starts with. After that, page down until you find the manufacturer's heading and click on the year of your target boat. Try to be as specific as you can in the next section, but any pricing information is better than none. The N.A.D.A. website allows you only five searches a day.

If a boat has been used in salt water, you should deduct 10 percent from the stated values on both boat and motor. In case you hadn't noticed, many values are for the hull only with standard features. You'll need to read carefully. A 1988 Mako center console is valued this way. You also have to search out the outboard motor value. There is a link on the Get Values Online page. Add the motor with any options you know the boat to have and remember to add for a trailer, if applicable.

I'm not singling out the N.A.D.A. guide for a special mention here: ABOS offers no website at present, and the BUC <http://www.buc.com/> site does not currently provide price information, except about purchase of their books.

Once again, take all of this with a grain of salt. Use your best judgment when viewing the boat firsthand, as you'll learn in the next section.

Shopping in Person

After spending time on the phone, you'll have the beginnings of the education you need to shop effectively. The common practice is to go out and look at all there is to see. This can be both time-consuming and frustrating. After you've viewed even 20 or 30 boats, they begin to lose their individuality and you may overlook the single, best deal for you. My suggestion is to narrow your choices on the phone and physically look at far fewer boats, the ones that are particularly suited to your wants and needs. With a little forethought, you can spend your time more effectively and get your best deal. Here are some shopping tips.

▣ **Make the time to shop.** Try to set aside an entire day for each shopping excursion (at least a few hours).

▣ **Take all of the decision-makers with you.** Do this if at all possible and bring your spouse, family, boating "expert," boating partner, and whomever else should be part of the decision.

▣ **Take along any tools you may need to do a cursory examination.** A tape measure, screwdrivers, flashlight, small mirror, and pliers are a good start.

▣ **Bring your notes and use them.**

▣ **Organize your shopping trip to cover one area at a time.** Driving all over the county is time-consuming, irritating, and distracting. Start where you feel you'll get the best deal and work your way down to the least desirable.

▣ **Allow the boat owner to talk—a lot.** This may be annoying, but the more he talks, the more likely he will begin talking about little problems he has had with the boat. Each problem has a negative monetary value and that's money in your pocket.

▣ **Try not to let emotion be your motivating factor.** The ability to walk away can save you thousands of dollars.

▣ **Take your time with each boat.** Do a thorough inspection. Don't let anyone rush you. Enjoy the day!

▣ **Be ready to commit to a purchase.** Notice that I didn't actually say *buy*. Great deals don't last long. A check ($50 to $100) given in deposit with the written understanding of a satisfactory sea trial should hold the deal for a few days, once you've negotiated.

I should mention here that one important factor to consider is your choice of a mechanic. I've found some of the best are in business for themselves as mobile mechanics. Call a few, tell them what you're doing, and ask for rates and references. If you have friends

Choose Your Mechanic Carefully

I once had a 225-hp outboard of my own rebuilt by a mechanic "on the side"—not at a reputable dealership. The fellow came highly recommended by a rich friend. I figured he must know his business if my friend Tom had hired him and didn't investigate any further. Wrong! The "rebuild" lasted two weeks and failed on Christmas Day with my new girlfriend and her son aboard. We managed to limp home; in the end, that $2,000 job cost me $4,500, plus a lot more down time. Always do a thorough check when looking for a mechanic.

with boats, ask them who they'd recommend. One or two names will probably keep popping up. You may choose to deal with a boatyard by using their mechanic. That laid-back boat salesperson can probably help you there.

You'll want your mechanic with you on the sea trial, if he can go. Even if it costs more, do it. It's better to spend a few dollars now than a lot of dollars later on repairs, for problems that will not be apparent on land can appear during the sea trial.

If you're in the market for a larger cruiser, you'll want someone with experience in generators, electrical systems, plumbing, and air-conditioning. Better yet: if you have truly narrowed down your choices to the larger cruiser you'd like to put a deposit on, now is the time to hire a surveyor. Remember that an outboard mechanic might not be very knowledgeable about inboard/outboards, and vice versa.

TIP

Let the seller talk.

The rest of this process is covered in the following pages. There is a fine line between jumping on a great deal and buying a boat too quickly and regretting it later. Trust your instincts, but always go through all of the steps.

The Boatowner

When you're approaching individual boatowners, always try to be friendly and relaxed. This will help them overcome a natural tendency to be wary of you. Deserved or not, each boatowner will have a certain amount of pride in his or her boat. Encourage this by complimenting something on the boat that you genuinely like (there is nothing worse than insincerity). Remember, the owner is your host and you're on his turf. The more relaxed both sides are at the beginning of the inspection, the more money you'll save. (Yes, I refer a lot to saving money; but that's why you're here, isn't it?) Introduce yourself and the people with you. Shake hands if you feel like it. Smile if you can.

All of these formalities are mentioned for a reason. You don't want to portray yourself as an adversary; you should come across as a friendly admirer. The boatowner is expecting you to downgrade his boat (thereby downgrading him) in order to get a better deal. I've seen boatowners go off like firecrackers when insulted by the mention of a defect in their vessels. Do the unexpected and avoid this altogether. The actual inspection method to accomplish this and, yes, save money, is covered in section 12, "Used-Boat Inspection: Checklist" (page 63). The owner is quite possibly more concerned about being denigrated by a stranger through his boat than about the bottom line he will accept. Understanding his motivations for selling is the key to finding the best bottom line.

The one who talks the most loses. Interesting thought, isn't it? In selling seminars, they teach you that the best ratio is for the salesperson to talk 30 percent of the time and listen 70 percent. This is good advice for buyers, too. Ask questions about motor maintenance, any major repairs, service intervals, options, extras, what's included in the sale and what's not, and so on. Get the owner talking and listen while you look around casually. He will want to tell you all about the positive aspects of his toy, or baby, or whatever he considers it. Please note that this is not the inspection phase. You will want him to talk until he is finished. Then follow up with some important questions. Write these down if necessary and pull out the list in front of him if you wish.

How long have you owned the boat? This is a strong indicator as to condition, motivation, and pricing. If he's owned the boat for only a short time, be cautious. If he reveals that he is just buying and selling like I was, he's in it for profit and the deal probably will go in his favor. He'll wait until he gets his price.

He may have recently purchased the boat and is having problems with it that he can't handle. This can be good or bad; a very careful inspection is warranted and, if you do buy the boat, a bargain basement price is what you want to pay. His financial picture may have just changed for the worse.

Perhaps he's had the boat for years, which is good. He will hopefully have maintenance records for your review. He'll be more likely to have stories to tell. Encourage this. The more he talks, the more you'll save. Listen carefully.

Why are you selling the boat? This is a bottom line question. His motivation to sell directly affects the price he will accept. Maybe he has already found another boat and must sell this one first, usually in a big hurry. Or he may have already purchased another boat and needs to sell quickly. He may just want to get rid of the boat (be wary). He needs the money. The owning partnership is ending. He may be tired of boating altogether. His children are grown and the boat's not getting any use. His children are abusing it (careful here). Whatever the reason, always assume that there is a little more to the story. Without prying, try to follow up with a few more light questions. Empathize with him. We have all shared similar experiences and can relate to each other's situations if we try. A few encouraging remarks here will get a friendly conversation going and help to ease the tension of the buyer-seller relationship. People always prefer to deal with friendly people if they can.

How long have you been trying to sell the boat? This is a strong indicator of price flexibility. If it has only been on the market a few days or if you're the first one to see it, he may hold out for a higher offer. If it has been for sale for a while at the same price, he may be ready to deal. If he has reduced the price and still not sold it, make sure that you do a very thorough inspection. There may be a physical reason for the boat not selling. Bargain pricing applies here.

A boat that has been for sale for a longer period (a month, for example) may not have been effectively marketed. If he has a high quality hull and never mentioned the brand name or model in an ad, he may have gotten poor response. This could represent an excellent opportunity to get a great deal on a great boat.

Have you had good response to your ad? This can be very informative. A lot of people may exaggerate about the response, but the bottom line is the boat is still there. He

TRAP

Never insult the seller's boat.

may mention that more people are coming to see the boat later in the day. That's fine. Talk to him about it. Has he had any offers? Any weirdos show up? If you can get him to talk about the others, he may share stories of low offers, abusive people, untimely appointments, no shows. He'll mentally review the sales process up to this point. Most people consider it a nerve-racking experience and want it to be over with. In doing this, we are continuing to set up the negotiation phase.

▣ **How much are you asking for the entire package?** Even if you already know the price, ask the question. Many times he'll say the amount and immediately state that he's looking for offers, or indicate in some other way that he's flexible in his price. If he comes back strongly with an aggressive I'm-firm-on-my-price stance, don't be discouraged. The game's only just begun.

Please note that I said package, not boat. At this point if he is not including certain items in the sale, they will be revealed. If he does withhold some items, this represents a negative monetary value to you as you were expecting a complete package. Keep this to yourself for now. Make a note of the item or items.

▣ **How did you arrive at that price?** Put the ball in his court. He will have to justify his price at this point. You will also get an insight as to the extent of his knowledge of the market. If the asking price was arrived at in a well informed manner, express agreement. If, on the other hand, his neighbor told him it should be worth that much, don't say a word and just look thoughtful. His next thoughts, if expressed, will probably be an indication of flexibility.

▣ **Are you firm on that price?** Unless you already have a strong indication either way, go ahead and ask. Less than 10 percent of sellers will risk offending you with a yes. Even if it is a yes, continue on with the inspection phase. If he feels that strongly at this point, you may have actually found a jewel worth having.

The Salesperson

Arriving at the dealership to see one or more used boats is challenging in itself. The boat salesperson is not quite as bad as the automotive counterpart, the used-car salesperson, but he or she is nevertheless there to sell you their products. He will represent his available inventory to his best advantage. Any flaws or shortcomings must undoubtedly be discovered by you.

When you arrive at the dealership, ask the person who greets you to find the salesperson you spoke to over the phone. Introduce yourself and remind him of your previous phone conversation. Tell him that you're pressed for time and would like to see the boats he mentioned over the phone. Once again, it's his job to control the sale by interviewing you at this point. Tell him the absolute minimum you need to be polite, and then go view the boats. An in-depth discussion on sales terms and strategies can be found in section 20 (page 107). A quick review of that material is helpful prior to your visit. Forewarned is forearmed, or something to that effect.

A quick walk around a boat is sometimes all that is necessary to ascertain an acceptable candidate for further scrutiny. Sometimes a salesperson will be overly generous in his assessment of a particular boat over the phone to get you to come out to his boatyard. If you find this is so right off the bat, thank him for his time and leave after a cursory inspection. If he has misrepresented basic facts to lure you out to his boatyard, what else will he misrepresent to sell you a boat? Keep on walking and don't look back.

TRAP

If a salesperson misrepresents a boat to lure you out to the yard, forget about doing business there.

If, on the other hand, you like what you see, pull out your notes and go to work. You should already have some basic questions answered about the boat. Now probe a little deeper. We'll take a moment to elaborate on the significance of the questions we asked him on the phone.

▣ **How long has the boat been on the lot?** This is a strong indicator of price flexibility, and the salesperson will hopefully be truthful with you. Has the price been reduced at all? Any offers at all on the boat? A lack of action after even a few weeks may indicate an excessive price tag. A recent price reduction indicates an increased desire to sell the boat and improves your chances at buying under low book value.

▣ **Is the boat on consignment or is it a trade-in?** He will have less of an emotional attachment to a consignment boat than a dealership owned trade-in. On a consignment boat, he is a mediator between you and the boat owner. He will get paid a commission, generally 10 percent of the sale price. He can try to get you to raise an offer or try to get the boat owner to take less for his boat. He probably doesn't have any more involvement than his commission, and he may end up more on your side in this situation. You make an offer, pointing out flaws. He then calls the owner with the lower offer and may try to convince him that it's in his best interest to accept. The boat owner may be paying a monthly storage fee to keep the boat in the boatyard, or he may be making loan payments. He may have a number of incentives to sell. These represent the best deals you will find on a used boat at a boatyard.

On a trade-in, the salesperson will be more involved. He may have taken it in trade as part of one of his new-boat sales and feels an obligation to sell it. After all, he may have convinced the owner or sales manager to take it in trade in the first place. He may well try to steer you to one or more boats of this nature. (When I worked at a used-boat dealership, 75 percent of the boats we sold were trade-ins and 25 percent were on consignment.) He is more likely to try to hold the line on a trade-in. He knows that the dealership has a substantial investment in this vessel.

Mechanical inspection, maintenance records, warranties, and a salesperson's sea trial are all important. If you're interested in a boat you will want as much of this information as you can get. However, nothing can replace your own thorough inspection.

◻ **Can you show me the book value on this boat?** Always get him to show you the value in the Blue Book. Read it yourself. Always. Remember, some boats sell better in certain areas than others. For example, in South Florida—where I have spent much of my boating time—fishing boats with outboards rule supreme. Farther north, in Michigan, a cruiser, cuddy, or bowrider with an inboard/outboard fetches the higher dollar. Your salesperson may have some insight into the local market to share with you and his interpretation of the book value is important. Just be cautious that he is not slanting his opinion towards his boats. I like to get a second opinion, and then a third.

This is still just the initial inspection phase, but you must judge the situation for yourself. Does this particular boat represent a great deal? Will it still be here next week? If you feel strongly about one, take time to do the thorough inspection described below. Use the touch-and-pause method as described in section 12, even with a salesperson. In the unlikely event he or she recognizes what you're doing, the worst thing you'll experience is silence.

If you feel at ease with this salesperson, get him involved in assessing the boat with you. The more he knows and will freely talk about, the better I feel. If he praises all that he can and always minimizes the flaws, he is working you, not working with you. Adversarial relationships with salespeople rarely end up working out in your favor. I have passed on some good-looking deals because I didn't feel right about the salesperson. I suggest you do the same.

Used-Boat Inspection: Checklist

Used boats should be inspected as thoroughly as possible. If you're like I was in the beginning, you're starting virtually from scratch. I recall that maiden voyage, doing 50 mph, flying over the boat wakes—until I came off an especially big wake and went right through the decking. Fortunately, I'm a little handy and it was easy to repair. That taught me to be just a little more thorough in my inspections. Use this chapter in conjunction with the information in section 2, "Boatbuilding 101" (pages 7–12) to weed out the lemons. Bring this checklist and use it as much as possible.

After the preliminary discussion and cursory examination, it's time to get down to business. Tell the owner that you're very interested (by now you should be interested or be gone) and ask him if he minds if you have a look around. Start in the stern, by the motor.

A method of inspection I learned from a used-car appraiser works well here. Keep the boatowner near while you inspect the boat by asking light questions as you go. Never criticize flaws, repairs, unusually installed options, etc. When you find that flaw, pause in your inspection, stop talking, and just look at it. Run your hand over it or touch it and let your hand linger there for several seconds and look thoughtful. Then, pull out this checklist and make a note. Don't say a word. Make sure he sees you do this, but try not to look at the boatowner (yes, you can look at the salesman). He will usually attempt to make light of the flaw by explaining the minor

TIP

Always hire a profes-
sional mechanic to
inspect the motor and
mechanical systems
of a used boat prior to
purchase.

mishap or circumstance during which
it occurred. If he does, just smile, nod,
and move on. No one will object to
your finding a flaw. They will only object if you attempt to beat them over
the head with it during the negotiation
process.

Do not discount the effective-
ness of this method! Think of it this
way: every time you touch a flaw,
you're putting $50 to $100 back into
your pocket. This method is taught to sales estimators by
nationally renowned sales trainers.

The following checklists should be used—along
with common sense—to help you decide whether or not
to pursue a particular vessel. Some items are relatively
minor and will not disqualify a boat, although we will use
them as bargaining points. Some items are deal-breakers:
if a boat with an outboard fails the transom test, you
should walk away.

I have indicated below which flaws are minor and
which are clearly fatal. The remainder fall somewhere in
between. If you find yourself answering yes to three or
more inspection queries in this category, you will need to
pause and appraise the situation. You will always hire a
professional mechanic to inspect the motor and mechanical systems prior to purchase, and he or she should be
able to sort out the flaws and answer your questions. You
have to decide whether it's worth going to that stage.

Engine and Propulsion Inspection

Refer to this master list when inspecting all motors and
before deciding whether or not to proceed with a fuller
and more detailed inspection by your mechanic. The boat
hull–systems section (page 69) will contain a few addi-

tional inspection areas. Most of these tasks apply to all
types of motors; the few items that are relevant only to
inboards (**IB**) or outboards (**OB**) or inboards/outboards
(**IO**) follow in a separate list.

For All Types of Motors

☑ **Check the prop.** Is it bent or chipped? Is the hub in good
shape? An aluminum prop in rough shape is a minor
item, but stainless steel props are expensive to repair or
replace. A clearly abused propeller can be unbalanced
and cause excessive vibration, which you won't detect
running the motor out of the water, with a garden hose
supplying cooling water.

☑ **Check the skeg and rudder.** On outboards and inboard/out-
boards this is the bottom-most fin on the lower unit and
serves as a rudder. Is it chipped, bent, or broken? If so, it
will likely require professional repair. Get an estimate.

☑ **Find the model and serial number of the motor.** The serial number
plate should be intact and located on the motor bracket
on an outboard, or on the top of the motor on an in-
board/outboard or an inboard. Copy down all of the information on this small metal plate. Different motor
manufacturers have different model codes that indicate
the model year. The marine mechanic must be able to
verify the model year for you prior to purchase. If you're
unable to verify positively the year of the motor, you'll
be taking a sizable risk in purchasing this boat. On a
used boat, the motor may well be worth half of the total
value of your purchase, or more.

☑ **Grasp the steering wheel and move it back and forth, all the way from
end to end.** Is there any binding? Is it easily moved? If the
system is difficult to turn, make a note for your mechanic.

☑ **Grab the throttle control and move it back and forth.** Is there any binding? If so, bring it to your mechanic's attention.

☑ **Ask the owner to hook up a water hose and start the motor.** Does the motor start easily? If not, make a note for the mechanic.

☑ **Make sure the water is circulating well.** The water cooling system is critical to the safe operation and longevity of the motor. This area requires careful inspection. Any obvious malfunction here is a deal-breaker. There should be a telltale stream of water shooting out from under the bottom on an outboard; I/Os and IBs should have water temperature gauges, and the temperature should be 180° to 200°F when running on a hose—a bit hotter than in normal operation, which would be around 180 degrees.

☑ **Does the motor idle and run smoothly?**

☑ **Make sure prop is clear and shifts from neutral to reverse, from neutral to forward.** Does the gearcase shift smoothly?

☑ **Do the gears work?** Are there any unusual noises? Lower unit work is a major expense.

☑ **Replace the engine cowling or compartment cover.** Do all the catches align easily? The hinges themselves are a small item, but replacing the cowling is a major expense.

For Specific Types of Motors

☑ **IB Check the prop shaft for obvious signs of abuse, corrosion, or wear.** If it's bent or worn or corroded, it will probably need to be replaced—at considerable expense.

☑ **OB** **Do a transom test.** With the outboard motor in the up position, grab the skeg and rock the motor up and down. Look for *any* flex or movement in the transom. This is an important inspection point for older boats. Any movement whatsoever in the transom structure indicates rotting wood inside the laminate and a major safety hazard. This is a clear deal-breaker.

☑ **OB** **Inspect the tilt motor casing.** This is usually located inside the motor bracket. Is there excessive corrosion? This could indicate a major repair in the future.

☑ **OB** **IO** **Inspect the lower unit casing for chips, cracks, or corrosion.** Minor chips and corrosion are acceptable, but cracks in the lower unit casing are a deal-breaker. Such cracks indicate that major repairs are needed: a cracked lower unit (gearcase) allows lubricating oil to escape and salt water to enter, which corrodes and degenerates gears and eventually causes a failure.

☑ **OB** **IO** **Use the control tilt/trim switch to raise and lower the motor.** Listen carefully. Does it operate smoothly? Do you hear any unusual noises? It should be just as smooth, even whine. Does it go up all the way? Any repairs needed here are quite expensive. If in doubt, wait and ask the mechanic.

☑ **OB** **IO** **Inspect the tilt/trim ram seals for leaks.** They should be perfectly dry. If not, another expensive repair is in the wings.

☑ **OB** **IO** **Tilt the motor halfway down and remove and inspect the engine cowling or engine compartment cover.** It should be noted that some I/O and IB engines have a separate, freshwater cooling system. Ask the owner before you open the engine compartment. If the boat uses a freshwater cooling system, have him show you how it works. Check the motor, or lower unit. It should remain halfway up and not drift downward. As noted above, repairs to the trim system are expensive.

☑ **OB IO Inspect the engine (powerhead) surfaces.** Is there any corrosion? Moderate corrosion is not serious, but it's an indication of overall maintenance. Is there any peeling paint? Some owners will do a quick repaint to improve appearances.

☑ **OB IO Look for homemade wiring splices.** If you find any, you should forget about this boat. Next look for fuel dripping or puddling under the engine (on an OB fuel collects in the front bottom area; on an I/O look on top of the motor block or in the bilge area). If you do find fuel under the engine, the most likely culprit is the carburetor, which is expensive to rebuild. Is the engine cool? Does it appear as if the engine has been started recently? (See more on this in the For All Types section.)

☑ **IO IB Inspect all belts, hoses and clamps for cracks, excessive wear, leaks or corrosion.** Belts and hoses are minor items to replace. But if such wear is a symptom of engine overheating (due to poor maintenance in general), it could be the tip of an iceberg. Make a note to ask the mechanic.

☑ **IO IB Inspect the bilge area for oil.** This area should be clean and dry. Any oil may have come from the motor (in the case of inboard/outboards or inboards) or from the hydraulic systems (steering or trim tabs). A small mirror can help you inspect for leaks or corrosion under the motor (a very costly repair) and deep into those unreachable recesses.

☑ **IO IB Pull the oil dipstick.** Is the oil clean, or black and nasty? Is it at the indicated full level? This is another indication of overall maintenance.

☑ **IO IB Go forward and turn on the blower switch.** This should acti-
vate a small fan used to ventilate the engine compartment of possible gas fumes. Outboard motors generally
are not equipped with a blower. A functioning blower is
critical from the perspective of safety but is not costly to
fix or replace.

I've asked whether the motor is warm or has been
started recently for a good reason. The motor may start
with difficulty and idle roughly when cold, so the owner
may start it before you arrive. This could be an indication
of carburetor, ignition, or starter problems. I always like to
cold start a motor before I buy. Ask the owner politely if
he has started the motor today. He may have done so for
a legitimate reason (for example, another prospective
buyer).

This list may sound complicated. But it represents only a cursory inspection. If everything appears in
order, you'll still want to contact a marine mechanic to
run some tests and accompany you on the sea trial. If
you have access to a good mechanic, a thorough visual
inspection will do until he or she can check the motor.
If the motor doesn't stand up to this preliminary inspection, you've just saved the cost of a mechanic.

Boat Hull–Systems Inspection

☑ **Check all gauges while the motor is running.** Make a note of any
that do not operate correctly. This is a minor repair.

☑ **Check all navigation lights.** Again, this is a minor repair.

☑ **Find the bilge pump.** Check the switch or switches: both the
manual switch on the console; and—if there is one—the

Bilge Blowers

A doctor I knew was the proud owner of a beautiful 28-foot performance boat. The boat had just been fueled, and he settled in for a brief cruise. He turned the key and a rather impressive explosion resulted. The rear engine hatches, each weighing about 250 pounds, were blown 15 feet into the air. Flames raced through the bilge and blew out the cabin doors. The entire deck was separated from the hull by 3 inches on the starboard side. He was badly shaken but miraculously unhurt. I got him off the boat and sat him down and called the EMTs. He was not very coherent, but after talking to him for a while I learned that he'd never felt it necessary to operate the bilge blower fan after fueling. I bet he uses it every time now.

automatic switch in the bilge, which will be a small, wedge-shaped float switch near the bilge pump. The pump should engage when it's pulled up. Like the ventilation fan, this is an important safety item but a minor repair.

☑ **Check the power to any electronics.** This is probably a minor repair, but it's a useful bargaining tool. Try out the electronics as much as possible.

☑ **Inspect the wiring inside the dash console.** Are there any home-made splices? Any loose wires hanging out or going nowhere? At the very least, bad wiring is an indication of poor overall maintenance and a prime source of system failure. It's also a real fire hazard. My policy is to walk away.

☑ **Do a visual inspection of all fiberglass surfaces on deck.** Are there any cracks? Minor cracks or crazing (hairline cracks that resemble spiderwebs) are unsightly, but they are not structurally important. As we saw in section 2 on boatbuilding, spider cracks on a newer boat may result from a gelcoat layer that was either too thin or too thick. Likewise, dis-

TRAP

Always be wary of rewiring.

coloration or blisters in the gelcoat of a newer boat indicate a poor-quality gelcoat. These are signs of an inferior manufacturing process. In an older used boat, crazing may occur due to stress or flexing and may not be the fault of the gelcoat. Crazing around the base of a cleat, for instance, indicates that the loads on it are not being distributed sufficiently and a sturdier backing block is required.

Larger cracks or evidence of delamination (separation of the layers of fiberglass) are deal-breakers. You may hear crackling or popping sounds when you tread on a delaminated area of the deck. An area of delamination will also sound different from healthy fiberglass when tapped with the butt end of a screwdriver or a small mallet. In a newer boat, this breakdown between the layers of fiberglass indicates poor quality control during the layup and will seriously compromise the integrity of the hull. Perhaps our technician didn't spend (or wasn't allowed to spend) enough time hand-rolling the fiberglass mat and resin of the first laminate layer. In older boats an initially sound hull can delaminate due to serious stress or water penetration. In either case, walk away.

☑ **Now for the fun part: jump up and down on every part of the cockpit and decks you can reach.** Do any sections feel soft? If so, this probably indicates that the stringer system we discussed in the boatbuilding section is wood and was not properly resined and sealed during installation. The wood has decomposed due to water penetration and no longer supports the deck—or, for that matter, the hull. On a boat with a soft deck, there's a good chance the transom is unsound as well (see the engine inspection checklist, above). They were installed and sealed at the same time, most likely by the same person. This is a deal-breaker.

☑ **Inspect the bimini top fittings and posts.** Are there cracks, bent poles, or missing straps? Is the canvas in good shape? Put it up and take it down. Do the same with any boat covers. These may sound like minor points but repair adds up.

☑ **Look carefully at the vinyl seats and bolsters.** Are they worn, torn, loose, or cracked? Is the backing made of wood? Is it solid or rotted? Believe it or not, seats and bolsters are so expensive to repair or replace that this could be a deal-breaker.

☑ **Are the seat bases loose, broken, rotting, or cracked?** Grab them and shake. This is a minor item.

☑ **Inspect all of the deck hardware.** Are there any corroded, cracked, or broken cleats, rails, latches, hatches, etc.? This is another relatively minor item.

☑ **Open every inspection port and look below.** Look as far inside as you can using the flashlight and mirror. Is any rotting wood visible? Poke around carefully with a screwdriver. If you see any sign of fiberglass delamination, walk away.

Examine the stringer system as well as you can. Are the stringers fiberglass or wood? If wood stringers are used, they should be completely encapsulated with well-resined fiberglass. Unsealed wood stringers will rot and fail to support the deck and hull. The same goes for wooden floors and decks.

Do you see any homemade wiring splices? Again, I would walk away. How about oily residue? Or an excessive fuel smell? If so, I would be careful. Make a note for the mechanic.

☑ **Look for evidence of recent work.** This could include: poor sealant application around the fuel tank access; newly installed carpet; newer fittings on fuel lines, hoses, pumps, and through-hull fittings; newly spliced wiring; fresh paint. If you find any of these, ask about them. Who did the work? Why was it done?

☑ **Do an exterior hull inspection.** Look for any cracks, chips, patches, or new paint, particularly near the rubrail. Larger cracks or signs of delamination are deal-breakers (see the deck inspection, above). New paint can hide a hasty repair. It's not uncommon to find that a fresh coat of bottom paint hides a rather large patch.

☑ **Find the hull identification number.** This is usually located on the stern just below the rubrail. Now is a good time to verify the year of the hull. The last two numbers of the year—76 or 89—will be located within the last two or three digits of the hull ID number. For example, "MTM24165M828" indicates a 1982 model year.

☑ **Examine the bow.** Follow it down to the first 3 or 4 feet of the bottom. Is the gelcoat worn through from beaching the boat? This is a costly repair and could have allowed water to enter the laminate.

☑ **Make sure the bow eye is intact.**

☑ **Is the rubrail bent, broken, or loose?** As you may recall from the boatbuilding section, the rubrail is where the hull and deck sections are fastened together on most boats. On such boats, the rubrail is crucial to the structure and watertight integrity of the hull. Look carefully: a rubrail can hide a multitude of sins. If the hull and hull-liner unit did not fit correctly when mated, the builder may have used an excessive amount of sealant to fill in the gaps. In this case, the fasteners may be exerting pressure to hold the joint together. When the joint is stressed, as in a rough sea, cracks and splits may appear and leaks will follow when the sealant fails. Look below the rail.

TRAP

Are the vinyl seats and bolsters in bad shape? Repairing or replacing them is expensive enough to disqualify that boat.

There should be a thin, even line of sealant. The more caulking I see, the less I like the boat. If it looks like water could enter through this joint, you must seriously question the seaworthiness of the boat. Invest in a hefty bilge pump if you buy.

By now you may have guessed my feelings about hack wiring, but I'll mention the point again. Always be wary of rewiring. If it was not done properly, this is a potential problem and even a safety hazard. Do you see wire nuts, or taped connections without solder, or barrel lugs? This smacks of a hasty repair and is a bad sign. Remember this book's creed: Don't buy someone else's junk.

Trailer Inspection

I like aluminum I-beam trailers the best, galvanized steel next, and painted steel the least. Larger trailers—dual axle, for example—should have at least one set of surge brakes. The front coupler is considerably larger because it houses the actuating cylinder. Surge brakes are great for larger boats. But unless the trailer is fairly new or recently rebuilt, they rarely work.

Bunk trailers are usually best for smaller boats, provided you have decent launching ramps close by. They hold up better and are easier to maintain. Roller trailers are great for steeper, shallower areas where ramps are of poor quality or nonexistent. However, they have more moving parts and require more maintenance.

TIP

Don't let a bad trailer come between you and a good boat.

A trailer can almost always be negotiated out of a deal, so it shouldn't become a deal-breaker. If you like the boat but the trailer is in bad shape, pursue the boat and get pricing on a new or nearly new trailer to replace it.

☑ **Look first for obvious rust or even rust holes.** Do you see any rusty U bolts? (These fasten the suspension leaf springs and axles to the frame and are usually the first to go.) Are the leaf springs rusty? Do you see any evidence of repainting?

☑ **Look at all of the exposed wiring.** Are there any homemade splices?

☑ **Are there any cracked or broken taillights?**

☑ **Check the tires.** Are they worn, cracked, or low or flat?

☑ **Does the trailer come equipped with buddy bearings?** These are grease fitting caps that fit over the hub on each wheel. A definite plus.

☑ **Inspect the wheels.** Are there rusty lug nuts, rims, or fenders?

☑ **Step way back and look for any sagging or a bent frame.** Do not buy such a trailer.

☑ **Visually check the brake lines where applicable.** Always ask if the brakes work.

☑ **Check the front coupler for obvious damage.** Does the locking mechanism move freely?

☑ **Check the identification tag.** Trailers come with an identification tag near the front where the "wishbone" meets. If this is unreadable, the owner should have a current registration with year model information on it.

☑ **Bearings and axles.** Unless you're willing to dismantle the wheels—or know someone who can—the bearings and axles will be impossible to check. I like to have the trailer and boat hooked up to my vehicle to take to the sea trial (see the final inspection, in section 14, page 85). Allow the seller to ride with you if he likes. Turn the radio and A/C off and listen. Concentrate and get a feel for the way the boat and trailer pull. When you arrive at the ramp, place your hand on or near the hub of each wheel. Are they hot? Hopefully not.

This may seem like a lot to do, but only a few boats will require the complete look over. Do not be concerned about doing a thorough investigation in front of the owner. He will object only if he has something to hide. Once again, do not criticize flaws. Ask legitimate questions about legitimate concerns. Keep it light. Don't make a big issue over little things.

After the first few inspections, the process will become a little more routine. I'd suggest doing a couple before getting serious about your purchase. You'll be more observant as you become more comfortable with the process. Repairs can be very pricey. Remember, all purchases of used boats without written warranties are "as-is". Verbal warranties are virtually unenforceable and usually not worth the paper that they're not written on.

On more recent models, ask the owner if there are any remaining warranties. You might get lucky. If you do get a yes, check it out. Not all warranties are transferable. If the seller presents a warranty as part of the package, you need to bring up the issue of transferability and have him show you how this may be accomplished. Many manufacturers' warranties are not transferable to subsequent owners. Extended warranties can be tricky to transfer, and there is usually a $25 or $50 fee to do so. Always read the fine print!

The Negotiation Process

Here's the part we've all been waiting and preparing for. By now you've determined that this may be the boat for you. You have looked the boat over as best you can and hopefully anything you haven't seen will be covered by the mechanic or during the sea trial. Any negotiations from this point on are subject to these two very necessary steps.

You and the seller should be getting along fairly well at this point, but there is a rising tension in the air. He or she sees that you like the boat and anticipates an offer, hoping not to be insulted or disappointed. You, on the other hand, are both excited and maybe a little nervous. How much should you offer? What should you say? Do you try to point out the flaws and justify your lower offer? Will he get upset? Will he laugh you off the property? It helps to have someone with you to use as a sounding board and to break away for a moment to get everything into perspective. If you're alone, you may want to go to the car. Just excuse yourself and go. Sit inside, if you like, and stare at the boat while you think. Do not attempt to justify your actions to the seller: just do it. It's important to break away from the boat and owner at this point.

This pause allows you to regain control of the moment. Slow down. Think. Relax. Smile. No one can be overly serious when they're smiling. Besides, if the seller sees you sitting in your car alone, looking thoughtful and smiling as you look at the boat, he'll relax too (or take you for a nut case and run into the house). Review your notes. You should have already determined before you arrived what you want to pay for the boat. You just want to present it in the best light. If the boat is extremely clean, you may want to bump up your offer, but not by much. Remember the most important rule: The ability to walk away will save you money, lots of money. Now, go out there and get that boat!

Approach the seller and tell him you'd like to make him an offer on the boat. Not his boat, *the* boat. Tell him that besides a few minor flaws, you really like it. Don't be afraid to let your admiration for the boat show.

Positively let it show. Tell him what you like about it. Compliment him on what he has done right with the boat. Express a small amount of reservation about what may be wrong with the boat, but indicate that these are probably only minor considerations. Your whole attitude should reflect that you're happy you've found this nice boat that you'd really like to buy, but. . . . Then simply tell the truth. How's that for originality?

You have promised yourself that you would spend only $ _____ for your used-boat purchase. (This shouldn't be your best bid, but close to it.) Tell him immediately that you feel his price may be a little high, but not by much. You can even tell him that if he holds out he may very well get close to his asking price, but you're prepared to deal now. You like the boat a lot, but you need to hold back some money for taxes, registration, supplies, whatever. You've been out shopping and know a quality boat when you see it, but can only afford to spend $ _____ . Now ask him: "What do you think?"

Then be quiet. Let him talk. How can he hate you when you've told him that you think he's got a great boat that is close to being priced right? If he has indicated earlier that he is firm on his price, he may still not bend. If he is standing firm and is not insulted, carry on!

Probably the first thing he'll say—this is the worst-case scenario—is that he could never take such a low offer for the boat. That it's worth what he's asking. He won't be offended. He'll still think well of you because you've been honest. This whole dickering process is usually based on nothing but falsehoods. You never said that you couldn't spend more: only that you promised yourself you wouldn't. He won't feel insulted because you've told him he is realistic about his price. You didn't try to beat him over the head with the boat's flaws; all you did was notice them. Anyway, back to the moment at hand: he has politely (or nearly so) refused your offer.

Walk around the boat. Poke around a little more. Look at him and ask him what he would take for a cash sale right now. Then be quiet and keep looking around. He'll probably drop no more than 5 percent. That is where he really wants to be—but not where you want to be. You're still way apart right now. Casually ask him what he thinks that minor repair over there will cost. Did he ever get an estimate? If you can, do that twice, but only twice. Let him do almost all of the talking. If there are no such repairs needed—in which case you've evidently found a really good one—ask him what it costs to register the boat. Or how much a new prop or Coast Guard–required gear will cost. Let him know by these little signals that you're trying to figure out if you can put the rest of the money together. But never say that! He will realize that you have a little money in reserve. That is a good thing.

Generally, the next thing most people try to do is split the difference. If you're that close, try it. However, I'm assuming in this example that you're still at least 10 percent away from a purchase—not to mention the mechanical inspection and sea trial that you have yet to bring up.

Look at him and say that you can come up with a little more money, such as $ _____ (whatever you had originally defined to yourself as your top offer). You realize that this is a little less than the $ _____ (the second figure he'd mentioned), but he can sell the boat now if he'll take your offer. He won't have to spend any more of his time putting up with people who might be rude, crude, or otherwise. Phrase that however you like, but you must say it. Also tell him that you're still shopping and actually need to go to see another boat when you leave here. You can even show him some of your notes. It's always good to have a boat ad with you, similar to his boat and priced less. I'd much rather have your boat, but the most I can really spend on it is $ _____ . That is cash available to me tomorrow. Once again say, "What do you think?" Then be quiet and let him talk. Yes, this is your final offer.

By now you've probably taken up at least a half hour of his time (the longer the better). He likes you and knows that you're the kind of person he'd like to see owning the boat—one who obviously wants to repair it and take good care of it. If you have spent the time well, he has had a chance to reflect on this whole process. There is a very good chance that he'll give in at this point and sell you the boat. You, after all, are ready to do business now. If he does, be happy. You've probably saved at least $1,000, and quite possibly more.

Should he stand firm and refuse your offer, don't despair, but don't raise your offer. If you've developed the rapport that you should have by now, hang out a while unless he indicates that he wants to go back into his house. (He won't; you're still there and interested, aren't you?) Talk a little about your experiences with boat shopping so far. Tell him about the good ones and the bad ones that you've run across. Talk about his boat when you can. Compare it favorably with boats you've seen. You can truthfully express regret at not being able to purchase his boat. He may ask you if you have access to any more money. Say yes, but that you cannot exceed your budget for the boat purchase, even one as nice as his. You'll just have to keep looking and hope you find something like this (then touch the boat).

I cannot tell you how many times telling the truth and handling the negotiation process this way has worked for me. I recall buying a small bowrider, very clean, that the owner had been asking $3,000 for. At that price, it would have been a pretty good deal in itself. I told him he had a great boat in fine shape, but all I had allotted to spend was $2,000. He refused at first, quite adamantly as I recall. Yet 20 minutes later, after some more light conversation (as I described above), we were driving off with that boat for $2,000. After having a few weeks of fun with it, I sold it for $3,250.

I could go on and on about many such deals. I picked up another little barnacle-encrusted bowrider for $3,500, after negotiating in a similar manner. The owner was at $4,500, and willing to back off a little to compensate for the bottom job. I bumped my offer marginally right near the end of our conversation ($3,500 was my top bid) and—after he reflected on the trials and tribulations of the whole sales process—he finally gave in. After doing a thorough bottom job, I sold it for $5,200—and that buyer told me himself that he was virtually stealing it from me! Again, we win. Let's proceed.

At this point, there are only two scenarios left. First scenario: the seller has finally agreed to accept your offer. Be happy! All of your hard work has paid off and you're on your way to owning the right boat, at the right price, the first time out. Here is how you should proceed.

Tell him you'd like to give him a deposit check and complete the deal at his convenience, perhaps tomorrow or the day after. A check for $50 or $100 should do. Of course, you'd like to have your mechanic take a quick look. Ask him if he minds if you write out a receipt and do so. Always make out a receipt to include

☐ his full name as the seller

☐ your full name as the buyer

☐ the date

☐ a brief description of boat, motor, trailer, and any other included articles

☐ the hull ID number

Ask to see the title at this point (if you live in a titling state, see page 88. If he doesn't have it at the house, it's okay. Casually ask where it is and if it's free and clear (no bank lien). Complete the receipt with

☐ the total amount of the sale

☐ total amount of the deposit

☐ balance due at closing

☐ a note that the deal is subject to satisfactory sea trial

It's not necessary to make the deal subject to satisfactory mechanical inspection. The phrase "subject to satisfactory sea trial" is ambiguous enough to offer you all the justification you need to back out of the deal if it turns out to have hidden defects (see the final inspection in section 14, page 87). You should place a definite time limit on the sea trial and closing. This will protect both parties from unreasonable delays. Of course, if you're unable to finalize the deal within the time period, you should be prepared to forfeit your deposit.

Ask the owner when you might be able to put the boat into the water to test it out. Try to leave the timing open and contact your mechanic. If the owner truly has a quality boat, he cannot object. If he does, ask why? Ask him (politely) if he drove his present car before purchasing it? It's the same thing. Insist that it's only a formality, but stand firm. When he consents, write out the deposit check and have him sign the receipt. Try to leave him with the least amount of deposit possible, but leave at least $50 to hold the boat.

Now for the second scenario. He cannot or will not accept your offer. If he still doesn't give in after you have pretty much talked your heart out—you'll know when to quit—it's time to go. This is the walking part. Thank him politely for his time, shake his hand, and ask him if he'd like to take down your name and number in the event that he changes his mind. He will take your number nine times out of ten, even if just out of courtesy. Explain that you probably won't be home for a couple of hours (this will reinforce the fact that you're going boat shopping). Tell him again that you feel he has a nice boat and wish him luck in selling it. Shake hands and walk away.

Then go out and look at the next one.

He who calls back first, loses. If you find yourself thinking the next day that perhaps you should have offered more, or that you really, really liked that last one, you're setting yourself up for a fall. If you call him, he has won and can hold firm on a higher price. If he calls you, he's indicating that he's ready to accept your offer, or one very close to it. Do not allow your emotions to creep in past your better judgment. Occasionally I've missed out on a great deal because I set my sights too high or my bid too low. But I can honestly say that the many great deals I have been able to make by using this system have overwhelmingly outnumbered the good deals that I've missed.

I wouldn't hold out too much hope for a return call, but consider this. If he doesn't get his price in the next few days, who will he be thinking about? You! The nice one. The one who didn't criticize his boat. The honest one. If he makes any calls, the first will be to you. In my experience the actual percentage of return callers was low, but these were great deals when they came through.

The Final Inspection

So it's now time to go back, with your cash or cashier's check in hand, to purchase the boat. If you do get a cashier's check, have it made out to yourself and then sign it over to the seller when you consummate the deal. Contrary to popular belief, this is not yet a done deal. You should call the seller to verify that he or she has time for the sea trial and contact your mechanic to coordinate the final inspection. Have that list of flaws ready for him to examine on the way over or once you arrive.

Introduce your mechanic to the seller and explain that you wanted him or her to come along for the ride. You may suggest that the mechanic might want to do a few tests while you and the seller look over the title, verify the money, check out the electronics, and so forth. Again, if he has nothing to hide, he'll acquiesce. If he objects, ask why. Tell him that to you, this is a great deal of money and you realize that you're purchasing this boat in "as-is" condition. Can he really blame you for wanting to protect your own interests? Besides, the mechanic is not here to pick out any little flaws: only to verify compression, spark, lower unit seals, and general operation.

This is the order in which I prefer to do things. Introducing a mechanic at the last minute may seem rude, but it rarely is. If you feel more comfortable mentioning a mechanic at an earlier stage, do so. Also note that by "verify the money" I mean show him the cash or check; I don't mean *give* him the money. The money changes hands at the last possible moment.

Now is the time to verify that everything that was to be included in the sale still is. I knew a new-boat dealer who would substitute inferior quality products— VHF radios, trailers, even head systems—at the last minute to save a few bucks. A new-boat dealer! Needless to say, his customer satisfaction rating was one of the lowest in the nation. Protect yourself. The best time to avoid any misunderstandings is at this stage of the deal. Have the seller show you those electronics, the life vests, the fire extinguisher, the anchor and line, and everything else you expect to be included in the sale. Get back on

TIP

Wait until the last possible moment before handing over the money.

board if necessary to verify visually that everything is aboard and operational. (Just because the fish finder is attached doesn't mean there's power to it!) Be as discreet as possible, but do not sacrifice thoroughness for that discretion. At this point, you should be all business.

Hopefully, the mechanic has completed his on-land inspection by now and has given you the nod. Should he discover something that he feels is a strong reason not to buy, excuse yourselves and go discuss it. We'll discuss the results of a negative inspection at the conclusion of this section.

Tell the seller that all is well (as you knew it would be) and hook up the boat to your tow vehicle for the ride to the ramp. If the seller insists on towing with his vehicle, go along with it. Ask him if you can ride with him. Have your mechanic follow you in a separate vehicle and observe the trailer from behind. As I mentioned above, you should turn off the radio, open the window, and listen along the way for any unusual noises from the trailer. Upon arrival, go back to the trailer and place your hand on or near the wheel hubs. Do they feel hot? Did your mechanic notice anything unusual?

Help the owner drop the boat in the water. If you're new at this, he may have some good advice for you here. Observe all that he does. You can even learn from his mistakes. Once launched, check out the following.

☑ **Does the boat float level when empty?** It may sound silly, but if the boat lists at the dock, it will list underway and be harder to handle. An inherent list could be due to a poor hull design or weight distribution.

☑ **Observe the start-up procedure.**

☑ **Check to make sure all the gauges are functioning properly.**

☑ **Are the warning buzzers working?** Some newer boats have low oil and overheat warning systems. You'll hear a chirp when the key is first turned. Ask your mechanic to check this. Water may be circulating, but not properly. The motor could be running hot without any obvious signs. If there is no temperature gauge or the overheat warning system is inoperative, you might never know a problem exists. You should keep this question in the front of your mind. Excessive heat is your engine's worst enemy. In the absence of a temperature gauge or an overheat warning, your mechanic should inspect the motor and check the temperature of the water passages or the risers. Ask the owner when the water pump impeller was last changed. If this was not done recently, set aside about $150 to have it replaced. Your mechanic can do the work later.

☑ **Do all of the lights work?**

☑ **Are all of the electronics working?**

☑ **Test the bilge pump.** This gives you the opportunity to see if the boat is taking on any water.

☑ **Does the starter sound strong?** Does it crank without hesitation?

☑ **Examine all of the fuel lines you can for leaks while the engine is running.**

Now take the boat out for a spin and take note of the following.

☑ **Does the motor idle all right under load (in gear)?**

☑ **Does the engine perform well at all speeds?**

☑ **Will the engine rev up to the proper maximum RPM?** Ask the mechanic.

☑ **Take the helm.** Does the boat steer easily?

☑ **Tilt the motor up partway.** Does it remain there under load?

☑ **How does the boat handle in a following sea?** Does it give a wet ride? If this is a big factor, talk about this with the owner. You have not yet purchased the boat. If you intend to go deep sea fishing and diving, this is important and may make you decide against the purchase.

☑ **Warn everyone aboard and then take it from three-quarter throttle to idle very quickly.** Look back. Does it take on water over the transom?

☑ **Shift into reverse gear.** Slowly bring up the throttle. Does it take on water over the transom?

☑ **How's the water circulation in the motor?** All outboards should shoot out a telltale stream of water (a pisser, for lack of a more delicate word). This should be a steady jet of water even at idle. An inboard/outboard or inboard should always have a working temperature gauge and not exceed 180 degrees.

☑ **Does the charging system work?** If there is a gauge, 13 to 14 volts is a normal reading; if there is no gauge, have the mechanic put a tester on it.

Again, some of these factors are important, some aren't. Your mechanic can explain the difference. If all is well, take the boat back in and be ready to complete the deal.

If you do not feel good about the deal after the sea trial for any reason, you're not obligated to go through with it. Rest assured that if you express second thoughts at this point, the deal won't go through. The seller doesn't want to hear anything except that you're going through with the deal. If you have doubts strong

TIP

If you don't feel good about a boat after the sea trial, you're entitled to get your deposit back.

enough to make you feel that this may not be in your best interest, walk away with your mechanic and talk about it.

Should you decide against it, do not hesitate to drop out of a bad deal and ask for your deposit back with your mechanic as a witness. The worst case is that the seller will refuse to return your deposit. Leave anyway; if you wish to pursue your deposit money, small claims court is your best answer. You have every legal document and a witness. You'll get it back.

Back to the satisfactory sea trial. Check the trailer again upon your return, with the boat off of it. Give the boat a last once-over and go inside to close the deal.

The Purchase

The majority of states are "titling" states. As is done with cars, a new title is issued whenever a boat is sold to establish legitimate ownership. The purchase can be fairly simple if the seller has a title with him. If you're unfamiliar with how the title should be filled out, do not mark it whatsoever! Call your state boating authority (see appendix 3, page 162) and inquire. One misplaced word can involve affidavits, extra trips downtown, and a lot of bad feelings. Many states still require a notarized signature, so you must take the seller and the title to a notary. You both then sign it, exchange money for title, and you're done.

If only it were always that easy. If you see a lien (evidence of money borrowed against the title), be careful. It should be very obviously printed on the face of the title. In a titling state, you should be able to bring the seller along when you register the boat and let the clerk verify the entire procedure. If there is an outstanding lien, an invalid title, or any of the ten zillion things that can be wrong, the state will find it. The seller may be carrying a lien on the title, and the title itself remains at the lending institution. This is fairly common. You must both go to the lending institution and satisfy the lien. You'll probably want to make an appointment. Always insist on a receipt here, even if you're entirely confident in the loan officer. If the title itself is at another branch, that's okay: fill out the necessary forms to have the title sent to you, and be prepared to wait for up to two weeks.

In nontitling states, the state boating agency is only responsible for administering the registration and numbering system. In general, a nontitling system does not afford you the same level of protection against buying a stolen boat or a boat bearing liens. A search by hull identification number (HIN) should tell you whether a boat is currently registered to someone other than the seller. Likewise, using the HIN you can check with the state police or the applicable agency to find out whether the vessel you're considering has been reported stolen. To detect a lien against a boat in a nontitling state you may have to go to a county courthouse or some other state office tasked with recording liens. Your first step should be to contact the agency responsible for recreational boating in your state (see appendix 3).

Always get a Bill of Sale. It's a wise thing to have this notarized also. If you get such a good deal that you have the state question it (they get fussy about sales tax), you have proof. The Bill of Sale should contain essentially all of the same information as your deposit receipt and should state "Paid in Full."

Return to pick up your new toy!

Maintenance Tips

You finally have the boat of your dreams! Now, besides having all of that fun, there are a few responsibilities that come along with owning this boat. Some regularly scheduled and performed maintenance should give you many years of trouble-free enjoyment. I suggest the following.

Before Each Use

- ☑ Install the bilge drain plug.

- ☑ Verify that the battery has a good charge.

- ☑ Inspect all your safety gear.

- ☑ Inspect the electronics; make sure they power up.

- ☑ **Inspect for any leaks.** This includes engine gas or oil, hydraulic fluid from steering or trim tabs, water from livewells or in bilge, and so forth.

- ☑ Open up the bilge area and aerate lower levels.

- ☑ Run the bilge pump to make sure it's working properly.

- ☑ Stow all gear properly.

- ☑ Visually inspect the motor.

After Each Use

- ☑ After use in salt water, flush the motor.

- ☑ Hose all dirt and salt from the boat, motor, and trailer.

- ☑ Clean the inside of the boat thoroughly.

☑ Remove the bilge drain plug (but not, of course, if you leave it in a wet slip).

☑ Examine the propeller for damage.

☑ Turn the battery switch to the off position.

Monthly or Bimonthly

☑ Spray down the engine block with a silicone-based spray to prevent corrosion. Try to keep it away from the carburetor intakes.

☑ Grease all grease points on the motor and trailer (gimbal bearings on an inboard/outboard).

☑ Polish and protect all stainless steel fittings and rails.

☑ Treat the vinyl with a preservative.

☑ Treat canvas with a preservative.

☑ Spray exposed electrical connections with electrical contact cleaner.

☑ Check the lower unit gearcase oil.

☑ Lubricate hinges and canvas snaps.

☑ Check belts and hoses (inboard/outboards and inboards).

☑ Check battery fluid level or levels.

☑ Check all lighting for bad bulbs, connections, etc.

☑ Check through-hull fittings for a proper seal. Check gate valves for proper operation.

☑ Check drain hoses and clamps.

100-Hour Service

One hundred hours is considered to be equivalent to one year of use.

- ☑ Tune the engine.

- ☑ Change the lower unit oil.

- ☑ Change fuel/water separator.

- ☑ Replace water pump impeller.

- ☑ Replace zincs.

Examine the following.

- ☑ hoses and belts

- ☑ fuel system

- ☑ warning systems

- ☑ oil pump

- ☑ trim/tilt unit

- ☑ steering system

- ☑ throttle system

- ☑ electrical wiring and connections

- ☑ screws, nuts and bolts (for tightness)

- ☑ bilge pump operation

- ☑ blower operation

- ☑ gauges

- ☑ all safety gear

- ☑ all lines

There are many other day-to-day and month-to-month duties to observe. The more complex the setup, the more to do. If you have air-conditioning, a generator, trim tabs, a raw-water strainer, a holding tank, a freshwater tank, a portable marine head, electronics, an automatic fire–extinguishing system unit, an inverter, dual batteries, and so on, these will need attention, too. Ask your dockmaster, salesperson, mechanic, or boating friend how to maintain your individual systems. Don't worry: boaters are by nature the type of people who'll give you all of the advice you'll ever need, and then some.

Buying a New Boat

PART 3

Buying a new boat is a challenge of a different kind. There are literally hundreds of new-boat manufacturers in the United States alone. These are loosely regulated and must meet only minimal safety standards. The variety of hulls and building techniques available is mind boggling. What we attempt to do in this section is provide you with some basic guidelines to follow in your search for a well-built, reasonably priced vessel.

There are no Big Three boat manufacturers, as there are in the car business. Indeed, there is an agreeably finite number of car manufacturers, foreign and domestic, which narrows down the choices nicely. The high cost of a dealership franchise keeps the number of dealers down, so competition, model selection, and pricing are well structured. Car model selection and price are usually our biggest concerns, after spending a little time studying consumer reports. But in recreational boating, we choose from countless models, hundreds of manufacturers, and erratic pricing. I have gathered brochures from only a small portion of the better boatbuilders, and there are 48 center console models between 18 and 21 feet!

I have seen the prices of a specific new-boat model with similar equipment vary as much as 22 percent. The boat I'm thinking of was a 23-foot center console model that was a particularly hot item in the fall and early winter of 1994. One sold for $20,900, another for $22,600, and another for $25,500—all within a few months of each other. You might see automobile prices vary by as much as 5 percent or $1,000 in a similar price range, but nothing on the order of $4,600. You will need to educate yourself before you can buy the right boat at the right time and at the right price.

The great number of boat manufacturers provides us with many buying opportunities. Competition among boatbuilders is fierce. A small boatbuilder may produce only a hundred boats annually, so every sale counts. They believe—and rightly so—that the more units sold and out on the water, the greater the exposure and possibility of future sales. Dealers rarely enter into franchise agreements with boatbuilders, so unit sales are critical if builders are to maintain their presence at the dealerships. Again the key word here is *competition*. The dealerships themselves are rebated by both boat and motor manufacturers for reaching certain sales plateaus. The dealerships make money on even marginally profitable sales. The pressure is on to maintain sales quotas if the dealer is handling a boat line of any quality.

This brings advantages and disadvantages. On the one hand, with all of the different manufacturers from which to choose, the market is deep. You may like boat A, which is built by a high-end builder and is too expensive for your budget. In this instance, with a little perseverance you may find one or more well-built boats B and C that are very similar to A but within your budget. On the other hand, you should always inspect boats B and C carefully to ensure that these are truly well-built, well-backed vessels. I say "well-backed" because a five-year hull warranty is only good as long as the manufacturer can afford to back it. When in doubt, ask around. If you hear bad things about the builder of B or C from several sources, it's time to consider other options.

I like to compare three to five similar boats from different manufacturers to establish the good, the bad, and

The new-boat buyer must think ahead. A cheap new boat is not a bargain if it doesn't hold its value.

the mediocre. The more you look at a particular style of boat from different manufacturers, the better chance you have of making the right choice.

Having read the opening chapters of this book, you have a good idea of the type and size boat you're looking for. Now we'll look at how to choose the right manufacturer and get the best price.

The new-boat shopper differs from the used-boat shopper in that his selection must satisfy his needs now and down the road for at least four or five years, particularly if he finances a portion or all of the purchase. He must choose carefully: an inexpensive price tag may have some appeal now; but after a couple years of use, our buyer may find that an inexpensively priced boat was a cheaply built boat and will not have a very generous re-sale value. I knew one person who, after making payments on a boat for over two years, owed over $7,000 more than the boat was worth! It pays to shop wisely.

I won't attempt to outline in detail which manufacturers I prefer and which I avoid. In appendix 2 (page 152), I offer a list of boatbuilders known for their quality—but that list is hardly exhaustive. My intention is that, when we're finished here, you'll have the tools necessary to make a determination yourself. You will be able to spot a poor-quality boat and avoid that trap.

For the average boater, a top-of-the-line boat may not deliver a good return on the investment.

You need to purchase a top-of-the-line boat only when you expect to be operating routinely in the worst sea conditions. Although these boats are always desirable, they are also pricey. It's better to find a good-quality boat that will meet and exceed your normal boating requirements. There are some great deals to be had out there, so let's go find them.

Shopping by Phone

In today's competitive market, shopping by phone is preferable to you and acceptable to dealers. It's a good way to begin and will save you lots of time and money. Most of today's salespersons are trained to be thorough on the phone, so go for it. If you like the person and boat information well enough, don't be concerned about giving him or her your name and phone number. The salesperson will undoubtedly reward you with a marked increase in cooperation. This process is a two-way street. A little cooperation on your end will save you hundreds of dollars on your eventual purchase.

Always take detailed notes of your phone investigations. Think of it this way: the more thorough your notes are, the more money you will save. Always include: the date of the call; the name of the dealership and its location, hours of operation, and phone number; the first and last name of the salesperson you spoke with.

Now for the specific questions. I'm going to focus on one model of boat for this questionnaire. I'll assume that you have very little knowledge of different manufacturers and how they rate. (That is how I began.)

▣ **What types of 18- to 21-foot center consoles do you carry?** They should offer at least two different brands.

▣ **What models do you have in stock?** (After all, you're not going down there to look at pictures!)

- **What kind of power are they equipped with?** The motor is a huge consideration. On some boats, it accounts for as much as half the total cost. Merely adequate power may not be enough when it comes to resale, so it's better to stay in the upper horsepower ranges (although not necessarily the maximum indicated on most boats and required on outboard boats under 20 feet).

- **What year is the boat/motor package?** Does he have any leftovers from last year?

- **What options does it come equipped with?** Make no assumptions here. What are standard options on most boats may be extras on others. Be as thorough as possible on this point. It helps to define the options you're looking for ahead of time.

- **How much does the boat/motor (and trailer) package, as equipped, cost?** Always ask how long the price is good for and whether the price is only good for that particular boat—that is, could a similar one be ordered in for you and would there be additional charges for freight and dealer preparation. Do not assume. Try to get a cash, out-the-door

Proper Equipment

Early one foggy morning I set out with some companions behind another boat to fish 30 miles offshore in the Gulf of Mexico in 3- to 4-foot seas. The other boat carried a loran; I had only a compass. The fog never did burn off. We got separated from the other boat and decided to head back in alone. Visibility was very bad by then, and full throttle reverse was the only thing that kept us off the beach when we found it. I couldn't make out any features on shore and had to ask a beachgoer which key we were standing off of. It was not the one I thought: I was at least 10 miles off course. As you think about options be sure that your boat is adequately equipped for the kind of boating you plan to do.

price. Don't be disappointed if you cannot obtain this on the phone, but try anyway. If you presently own a boat and the dealer asks about trading in, tell him you're selling your boat yourself. You can change your mind later, if you choose.

▣ **Have you run one of these models personally?** Nothing beats hands-on experience.

▣ **How does the boat ride in a rough sea?** Of course he will say, "Great!" Look for specifics here, not generalizations. Does it have a wet ride? How long does it take to get up on plane? Is the boat model on your lot underpowered? Will it need trim tabs? Does she "corner" well? Is it tender in a beam sea (waves hitting you broadside)?

▣ **On a scale from 1 to 10, how does the boat rate overall?** Naturally he'll be generous in his estimate, but a 9 or a 10 rating is definitely worth seeing. Again, make him qualify his answer.

▣ **Which model would you buy for yourself?** (Get him personally involved.)

▣ **What is the best boat to which you can compare it?** He'll probably name a more expensive line of boats. Ask him to explain why.

▣ **I've also been looking at XYZ brand boats.** What do you think of those? If he downgrades the other brand, make him be specific. He may not want to come out and say anything negative (the sign of a good salesperson, since telling you that you're looking at junk is the same as telling you that you're stupid), so probe and get some opinions.

▣ **How are these boats built?** Are they built with wood or fiberglass stringers? What about the decks and transom? Is the fiberglass hand laid or was a chopper gun used? Is the deck hardware through-bolted? Does the boat have full foam flotation? If he hedges here, you may be talking to the wrong person or about the wrong boat. He may not be educated about the building process used for that boat line. The other possibility is that he knows it's substandard and the less said, the better.

▣ **Is the hardware top-of-the-line stainless steel?**

▣ **How would you rate the fiberglass work?** The fit and finish?

▣ **Will it hold up well over the years?**

▣ **Do the hatches fit tight and straight?**

▣ **What's the standard hull warranty?** Is it transferable? What about the motor warranty? (See the section on warranties, page 130, for more information.)

▣ **How long has this manufacturer been in business?** Obviously, the longer the better.

Be creative. You don't need to ask all of these questions every time, and you may have your own questions to add. If the salesperson cannot or will not answer your questions, try to call back and talk to someone who can or will. If he's the only one there, you may want to call another dealership for information.

Now you'll be able to put pricing and options together. This entire series of questions is geared to help educate you on the dealer's boat models, his opinions of other boat models, and the caliber of salesperson you're dealing with. He may not appear to be well informed. That's all right. You'll appear well informed by asking the right questions. If you like him, allow him to call you back with any information about which he is in doubt. Any opinions you gather at this stage should be taken for just what they are: opinions. Many salespeople make unjustifiable claims.

TIP

If possible, buy a new boat from the local dealership—they will probably perform any repairs covered by warranty.

I prefer a salesman who substantiates his statements by looking up the information and calling me back.

Keep your notes in a file folder. If possible, have the salesperson send you a brochure and some notes on pricing. If they won't commit to a bottom line price, it's OK. Just ask for a ballpark figure. The more they cooperate at this point, the more likely they are to negotiate down the line.

You may expect them to make a follow-up phone call. This is always to your advantage. They must, at this point, offer you some additional incentive to buy. It's almost an unwritten rule. Put the salesperson on hold, find your notes, and go to work. It's easier to practice negotiating over the phone as opposed to dealing face to face.

Do not make a commitment at this point. If you like what you hear, tell them you may stop in later on in the week to check things out. That is plenty of commitment as far as your salesperson is concerned. If you feel like making an appointment (if they are any good, they'll ask), do so. If you don't, don't.

A good place to find new-boat dealerships in your area is the Yellow Pages (look under Boat Sales or Boat Dealers). If your area is served by a boat trader–type magazine, this is a great tool for finding out-of-town dealerships and comparing base prices. The Internet offers a wealth of information about new-boat dealers. Before going to an out-of-town dealer you should consider the consequences if a local dealer is available. Shopping one against the other will save you money. However, if you buy out-of-town, be sure that the money saved is enough to cover the hard feelings you may create with your local dealership. You'll probably have to depend on them should you require any warranty work. This is a tough call. I like to be up front with both sides. If your local dealer comes close to matching the out-of-town price, deal with them.

Pricing

There seem to be a great number of sales, shows, special events, clearance discounts, and who-knows-what-else to justify price changes in the boating industry. Prices seem to change weekly, and the competition for your boating dollar is fierce. This is a good thing, and we will use it to our advantage when the time comes. You can do a little research to find the lowest price before you leave the house.

As I've said, the trader magazines are a great resource and are a favorite among dealers. Here you will find pricing information on your targeted boats from more than one dealer. You're not necessarily looking to leave town for a better deal: what you want is some ammunition to use at your home dealership. He cannot refuse to match or at least approach a competitor's ad for the same boat. If he claims that the competitor's ad is misleading, ask him to prove it. Always insist that you'd rather deal locally, with his dealership, but you do not want to end up paying too much in doing so. No one can begrudge you that.

Now here's some insider information.

TIP

A typical markup from dealer invoice cost to MSRP is around 30 percent. Average markup on actual sales is 18 to 22 percent. A great deal is buying at 12 to 15 percent above invoice.

☐ **The low-to-average markup from dealer invoice cost to determine MSRP (manufacturer's suggested retail price) is 30 percent.** I've rarely seen boats marked up less. I have seen some marked up to 35 percent. For example, if your target boat is listed at $19,995 MSRP, divide this figure by 1.3 to establish the approximate invoice cost of the entire unit, options and all. Your answer: $15,380.76. Rarely will you be low on the invoice figure; more often the dealer will have a larger markup and the boat will actually have cost him a little less.

▣ **Most boat options (bimini top, extra cushions, larger motors) enjoy a similar markup.**

▣ **Most lending institutions recognize a 35 percent markup over invoice as their benchmark to determine loan value.**

▣ **Trailer sales are usually very competitive and are marked up substantially less, more like 10 to 20 percent.**

▣ **The national average of actual sales shows a markup of 18 to 22 percent actual gross profit over invoice cost.** The actual percentage varies from state to state.

▣ **Virtually every dealership "floor plans" their inventory.** This means that they do not pay for their boats up front; they finance them. The larger manufacturers generally prepay the interest for seven or eight months, so the dealership has from August to April or so to sell their boats (depending on when they arrive on the lot) before they have to start making monthly payments. The idea here is that the dealerships will place larger orders for boats at the beginning of the model year. The dealerships will try to hold the line on pricing for the first six months or so and then reduce prices as the payments get nearer.

▣ **You'll save money by ordering a boat from the factory between August and October.** Virtually every manufacturer offers the dealership a discount on boats ordered for cash purchase. This percentage, which is highest in August and lower after that, can be as high as 8 percent or more to start. Ordering a custom boat should cost you less, option-for-option, instead of more. The dealership will never pass this discount along to you directly. But as we shall see, it can be used later, when all else fails, as a bargaining chip.

▣ **The best time to buy off the lot is at the end of the model year (May through July).**

▣ **The best days to buy are one of the last days of the month, when dealers are getting anxious to fill their monthly quotas.**

▣ **New boats usually come out between July and August.** If you're buying a 1997 boat in May 1997, your boat is technically almost ready to celebrate its first birthday. When buying under these circumstances you should enjoy a nice markdown from the manufacturer's suggested retail price (MSRP).

▣ **Freight and dealer prep are real expenses.** These may or may not be included in the MSRP figure. Always check on this up front. As one would expect, freight and dealer prep costs are generally tied to boat size. For a boat of 21 feet or less, an estimate of $1,000 for these costs should be close, if not high.

▣ **You may encounter mysterious "service fees."** This can sometimes be as much as $500, which is tacked on by the dealership to increase gross profit. If pressed, they might explain these "services" as boat polishing or boat transportation within the yard. Be skeptical. In the worst case, you're being asked to pay for their overhead twice. Not many dealerships will blow a deal to keep this fee on the contract.

Keep these thoughts in mind when you're shopping. There are some great deals out there. A great deal on a new boat is buying at 12 to 15 percent above invoice. Very rarely will a dealer sell for less, no matter what the circumstances. They will almost always take a cash deal at 20 percent. Remember that buying a new, one-year-old boat (leftover) should be closer to invoice cost. Compare that leftover with the newer model and make your determination from there. Remember to investigate freight and dealer prep costs.

TRAP

Freight and dealer preparation are significant expenses. Always determine whether or not these are included in the MSRP.

Some dealerships have what are considered to be higher end products than others. These boats are more in demand (you might compare them with a Mercedes or a BMW), and dealers will not discount them much at all. You need to decide if a status symbol is what you're looking for. If so, don't be surprised when you're told that this is the price, take it or not. Many times a different manufacturer has a similar boat at substantial savings.

Additionally, some dealers are discount dealers. If you're browsing through the trader magazines and find that your local dealer is always priced substantially lower than the competition, your job just got easier. He'll not bend as much, but you can be confident that you're starting out much closer to your goal. Remember to research carefully before you go shopping.

The purpose of this discussion is to help you determine pricing by utilizing the above thoughts. You should avoid confronting a dealer with this information directly; the best use of this information is right at home, prior to your first call or after your initial visit to the dealership.

Shopping in Person

You should approach face-to-face shopping for a new boat much as we did with used boats. Turn to page 53 and review the in-person shopping techniques. Most of the points I stressed in that section also apply here. To recap:

☐ Narrow your options on the phone and inspect fewer boats with fresher eyes.

- ▣ Set aside a block of time for a shopping excursion.

- ▣ Take all of the decision-makers with you.

- ▣ Bring the tools you'll need to do a cursory examination.

- ▣ Bring your notes and use them.

- ▣ Organize your trip to cover one geographic area at a time.

- ▣ Try not to let emotions be your motivating factor.

- ▣ Do a thorough inspection of every boat.

When a new boat is the target and a professional salesperson is your contact, I would add the following suggestions.

- ▣ **Always be friendly with the salesperson who approaches you.** When applicable—which should be almost every time, if you've done your phone work—ask for the salesperson you spoke with over the phone.

- ▣ **Never commit to purchasing a boat on the first visit.**

- ▣ **Always let the salesperson know that you're ready to buy within the next few days.**

- ▣ **Don't be distracted by sales, special offers, or boat show prices.** Nine times out of ten, the deal will still be available up to a week later. When in doubt, let the salesperson know that you will not buy today and ask him to extend the sale price for a week. An unreasonable refusal indicates an unreasonable person.

- ▣ **Allow the salesperson to talk a lot.** It can be annoying, but the more he talks, the more money you'll save. It's common-place for the salesperson to assume that your silence in-dicates disinterest. He will feel uncomfortable and begin to offer incentives to buy.

▣ **Bring this book along and refer to it often.** There's no need to keep it out of sight. If they'd like to see it, show it to them. Knowing that you're an educated consumer will both impress them and show them that you're a serious buyer.

The Salesperson: Training, Terms, and Tactics (or, What the Heck Are They Teaching These People?)

Let's try to look at things from a salesperson's viewpoint for awhile. This will help you to understand his goals, strategies, and techniques. He wants to sell you the boat. Today's best salespeople are well trained and have an agenda from the opening hello to the thank you letter at the end. He also knows approximately what bottom line price the sales manager will quote you on the boat in question. He's probably already sold a few of them.

We'll work on the assumption that you will be dealing with one of the really sharp salespeople. That way you'll be prepared to handle the best, and anyone else will be that much easier.

TRAP

Special, limited-time offers don't expire as quickly as the sales-person wants you to think they do.

Modern sales psychology calls for the salesperson to become your friend, to empathize with you and discover your wants and needs in order to sell you a boat at higher profit. You may overlook the higher price because the sales process has been unforeseeably warm and friendly. Well, two can play this game. Always focus on the bottom line and limit your emotional

TIP

Focus on the bottom line and limit your emotional attachment to the boat and the salesperson. You'll win every time.

attachment to the boat, the person, and the dealership. You'll win every time. Remember, when negotiation time comes, the ability to walk away will save you thousands of dollars.

Training seminars teach salespeople to control the sale. Salespeople lead you toward the sale down a predetermined path with a specific program in mind. Some of what they are taught has to do with recognizing body language. But much of it has to do with one-liners. Yes, one-liners—lines and turns of phrase used as a segue to propel you towards the sale. Many such lines begin with, "No problem." Or, "If I could, would you?" And end with, "What do you think?" There are power greetings, ways to overcome objections, and about a zillion great closes.

The salesperson may want your first meeting to go something like the scenario described next.

Meet and Greet

▢ **You'll be greeted.** He or she will welcome you, shake hands, and tell you their name, wanting—by example—to get you to tell yours.

▢ **He'll ask, "What can I show you today?"** ("May I help you?" is for amateurs), half-expecting you to say you're just looking. He'll have a line for that, too.

▢ **He'll escort you to the boat or boats, perhaps asking if you're familiar with the manufacturers.** Then he'll give you some background information.

▢ **If he's good, he'll make a comment on something about you or your vehicle to get the conversation down to a more personal level.**

Wants and Needs

☑ He should ask you what your main interest in buying a boat would be.

☑ Why would you this particular type of boat?

☑ Perhaps he'll ask you if you're married.

☑ Do you have a family? (It's starting to sound like that questionnaire, huh?)

☑ Do you have a specific price range in mind?

☑ Are you looking to stay at a specific payment?

Show and Tell

☑ **Now comes the walk-around to show you the features and benefits of the boat.** He should start at the stern and work his way around the boat. You'll be shown the motor, its components, and it's benefits. Next the hull and its lines, the handling characteristics, the construction techniques, and how this will benefit you. This will hopefully take no longer than five to seven minutes and should be very informative.

☑ **You'll be invited aboard.** More features and benefits—all very informative and geared to find out what tickles your fancy, floats your boat, makes your day.

☑ **He should then go directly to those key points that pique your interest and emphasize their benefits.** These are called *hot buttons*. He'll be pushing these later.

Trial Closes

Trial closes are specific questions geared to determine how close you are to buying and to get you used to the idea of buying.

▣ Do you feel this is the right boat for you and your family?

▣ Is this boat in the right price range?

▣ What is your timeframe for buying a boat?

▣ If the price was right, would you buy the boat today?

▣ Wouldn't you just love to bring your family out on this boat?

▣ Remember the options you liked so much? This one has it all!
(He's pushing one of those hot buttons here.)

▣ Your wife said she loved the safe seating for the children. Don't you?
(Again, the hot-button technique!)

The Close

▣ Let's go inside and crunch some numbers.

▣ If you want the best price, I can get it for you. But my sales manager will want to know that you're ready to buy now.
Are you?

▣ If I can get you the right price, will you buy the boat now?

▣ If I can get you the right trade-in value for your boat, will you buy the
boat now?

▣ Is there anything besides price stopping you from buying the boat now?

There're about a million things, or was that a zillion?
Answer affirmatively and you've just bought a boat, perhaps before you're really ready.

He'll deny knowing the best price. He'll need a
written commitment with a check to approach his boss.
He knows he can offer it to you for $ _____, but that's
all he knows. His job is to make sure that you have chosen
the right boat for you (perfect lead-in for one of those
closes, right?) and his boss will get you the best price.

The point I'm trying to make is that you're probably going to be dealing with a professional. He'll want to be in control. That is what all of his training and techniques and one-liners all boil down to.

Recognizing this is half the battle. The best tool you have here is disinterest. You like what he has, but it's just not quite right for you. It may be adequate for your needs, but you aren't really excited about it. You appreciate all of the information, but you need to shop a little more. Keep him at arm's length, don't get excited about his product, and don't commit to anything. That way, you'll retain control.

The Dealership

Now that you're armed with some insight into the tactics of a salesperson, you're ready to visit the first dealership on your list. Arrive with your notes in hand and look for the boat or boats you inquired about over the phone. A salesperson will, no doubt, eventually approach you. Ask to see the person listed on your notes. If he or she isn't there, at least you tried. Continue on to your boat selection and proceed.

Ask the salesperson to identify the boats listed in your notes. You'll want to take your time and chat with him awhile. That is probably the last thing he expects. Most consumers want to be left alone during the initial inspection phase. We want him to relax and talk about the boat.

Ask again how much the boat costs. You probably already know, but the idea here is to have him commit to this price again. If there is a discrepancy in pricing between what you'd been given over the phone and what he tells you now, it will probably be in your favor. It's common for a salesperson to give up to a thousand dollars off of list

TIP

A salesperson is normally not allowed to drop the price more than 10 percent for a cash deal.

price in the initial face-to-face meeting. Each salesperson usually knows the maximum discount that he can offer you and may try to gain your interest by doing this. If he doesn't offer a discount immediately, tell him you're on a strict budget and ask for his lowest price.

He may ask about your trade-in. If you in fact have one, tell him that you intend to sell it yourself. This will be a cash deal. Would he mind looking up your boat in his Blue Book and letting you know what its approximate worth is? This is very important. Stop everything right there if necessary and get those figures. Have him write the numbers down on the back of one of his cards and keep it for future reference. If indeed you want to throw in the trade at a later time, you will probably get only the lower, wholesale figure from him. If you feel you can live with that (and still get that new boat at 15 percent over cost), carry on.

If you're preapproved, tell him that (see appendix 1, "Financing 101," page 144). Get him excited at the prospect of having an interested, qualified buyer right here and now. Remind him that you're out shopping for the best deal you can find on comparable quality boats. He'll probably get you his best bottom-line price right there. You can compare it to your estimated bottom-line price later.

What you're trying to do here is retain control of the buying process. If your salesperson is any good, he'll try to get it back. You've just gotten him interested in you and now he'll try to work you. Not work with you: work you. When he starts to probe, just get interested in the boat and begin walking around it, possibly asking questions. Do not allow him to interview you. The more he knows about you, the more control he gains over the sales process. If you're showing interest in the boat, he'll stay interested enough and you'll retain control.

Do allow him to show you a few similar models. But if they are not to your liking, tell him immediately and return to the ones that interest you. You might ask him if he's expecting any new models to arrive within the next couple of weeks. This will imply to him that your interest in what he has is limited, at best. It also tells him that you're buying within the next two weeks. Compliment him on what he does have, but don't get too enthusiastic. Make him attract your interest later with further buying incentives.

By now you should have a price for the boat that is $800 to $1,000 below MSRP. You've only just begun. As a rule of thumb, the total that a salesperson will probably be allowed to drop his price is around 10 percent for a cash deal. It's reasonable to assume that the salesperson does not know the bottom line; he'll have a good idea, but in the end it's not his decision to make. That is the job of the sales manager or the owner. Your goal will be at least another 5 percent drop, but save that for the return trip. At this point, you're still just looking at the different models he has in stock and trying to determine if any could be right for you. If he goes the entire 10 percent right away, you can bet that your return trip will net you that other 5 percent, maybe more.

Boat sales differ from car sales in that, for the most part, the salesperson will not try to hammer you into purchasing on the spot. This is a good thing. You'll almost never get the best deal on your first trip. This trip is for information gathering and giving the boat a good once over to get a general idea of quality and style. Get a brochure and have him mark down his best price. Ask if he has any information sheets that describe the boat as equipped on the lot. Get as much information as possible on the boat or boats you're interested in. Get his card, thank him, and leave.

Most salespeople will not even attempt to get your personal information. If he asks (and you like the way he's treated you thus far), consent to giving him your name and phone number. If he calls, it will be to offer you some further incentive to purchase his boat. He will also be a good sounding board (albeit somewhat prejudiced) as to the quality of other boats you're looking at. It's good to have a friend in the business. He may be willing to bring out that Blue Book for used-boat pricing if you need it.

Shopping Boat Shows

Did we just say that the salesperson probably won't try to pressure you into an immediate purchase? Here's where the rules change. Although a boat show is an excellent opportunity to compare different manufacturers and models, it's also hammer time! You'll have everyone from salespeople, sales managers, owners, and manufacturer's reps attending to you at each booth. They're pumped up and out there to sell or die. Every square foot of floor (or dock) display costs each dealership a good deal of money, and each dealership wants results.

TRAP

Boat shows are designed to excite emotion, and emotion will cost you money.

The key here is to be low-key. You're just looking and want the brochure. You'll be buying in a couple of weeks, but not today. Ask the salesperson his or her name and be friendly, but you've got a lot of ground to cover and want to see it all. You may be back later and, if so, you'll ask for him.

Don't be concerned about factory incentives or special pricing. If these truly represent a significant savings, chances are that the deal will still be available for at least the next few days at the dealership. If that particular, discounted boat sells, chances are you'll save money ordering one from the factory as long as you're willing to wait for it to be delivered.

Believe it or not, chances are that you're likely to pay more for a boat at a boat show than you would if you purchased later on at the dealership. I've seen it time after time. The excitement overrules our better judgment. It becomes an emotional sale, and you lose. The attraction here is strong, the lifestyle seems so appealing, and the temptation to believe what you hear instead of what you know is almost irresistible.

Sure, there are some boats out there that are bona fide deals. These are generally leftovers or hard-to-sell items (and therefore less desirable) that the dealership would like to see go away. My suggestion is that you do your price shopping before you hit the shows, and not at them. Boat shows are best suited for model and manufacturer comparison only.

New-Boat Inspection: Checklist

On a new boat, you're not looking so much for flaws (although these should certainly be noted); your goal should be to assess the quality of the construction. Many of today's manufacturers are more concerned with quantity rather than quality. Here is some more food for thought.

☑ If it looks cheaply built, it probably is.

☑ If you feel it's overpriced, it usually is.

☑ If it seems too good to be true, it definitely is.

☑ If you find cracks, bubbles, bad wiring, or loose hardware now, it will only get worse later.

☑ **A new motor should run perfectly.** If it doesn't, don't buy it— even if they fix it.

☑ If it seems too small for you, it is.

☑ Talk's cheap: get any promises made on paper.

☑ If the dealership doesn't take care of you during the sale, they never will.

☑ A new boat should be delivered detailed and waxed.

☑ Always get your warranties in writing.

☑ Always conduct a sea trial.

Things to Look For

Review the "Boatbuilding 101" section (page 7) and then examine the following.

☑ **Exposed or painted wood above or below decks.** Open up all of those inspection plates. Even if it's not directly exposed to salt water, unprotected wood will eventually rot. Be sure that any holes drilled in the decks or in the transom have been properly and completely sealed.

☑ **The stringer system.** If possible, look below and examine the stringer system. Are the stringers fiberglass or wood? If wood stringers are used, a marine fir is preferable to ply-wood. Wood stringers should be completely encapsulated with well-resined fiberglass.

☑ **Wiring and electrical connections.** Is there any exposed or corroded wiring and/or electrical connections? Wiring should be neatly run and well protected from accidental contact. All connections should be sealed with liquid electrical tape (applied with a brush) or a comparable heat-shrink tape. Corrosion causes loss of conductivity and systems failure.

☑ **Are there any obvious rough edges or unfinished fiberglass above or below decks?** Look for poorly cut openings for hatches, inspection plates, etc. Are there areas with an obviously poor finish? Raw edges of fiberglass above or below decks indicate inferior quality and workmanship. Look lengthwise down the side of the boat hull. Is the hull body wavy? If the sides of the hull are obviously wavy, it's a strong indication of a rushed job (the layup has not been allowed to cool sufficiently between layers). Slam the hull near the center with the heel of your hand. Does it feel solid?

☑ **Do you see any cracks, bubbles, or discoloration in the gelcoat?** This could indicate poor mold preparation, uneven gelcoat application, inferior quality gelcoat, or voids or flaws in the underlying laminate. This is bad news—any way you look at it.

☑ **Is there any moisture present in the gauges?** Foggy gauges? It doesn't matter who manufactured them. They'll never clear completely (even with the dash lights on). Get them replaced or don't buy.

☑ **Feel the steering.** Move the shift control. Is either stiff? Believe me, it's as good as it gets right now. Cheap hardware and poorly designed systems only get worse with time.

☑ **Is there loose, corroded, cracked, or ill-fitting hardware on deck?** Check windshields and railings too. If they neglected to use good-quality hardware in plain view, what did they use in places where you can't see? If possible, you should also try to get under-deck access to see how deck hardware

was fastened. High-load fittings such as cleats should be
through-bolted (not screwed) with big washers or metal
or wood backing blocks underneath.

☑ **Do the hatches fit well?** Do they creak, pop, or groan when
you step on them? This is a sign of bad molds or poor
quality control. Slight imperfections are acceptable; obvious flaws need replacing before you buy.

☑ **Is there any surface rust on the stainless steel hardware?** Already?
There are many grades of stainless steel fittings. A new
boat should show no signs of rust. I've seen 5-year-old
boats used in salt water with no obvious rust. Did they
cut corners here? And where else?

☑ **Do you see any obvious saltwater corrosion on exposed metal?** Check
any exposed aluminum frameworks or rails, the alu-
minum strip where the windshield meets the console,
the sacrificial zincs. If you find corrosion, the boat has
probably been used as a demo. Believe me, there are very
few demos out there that have only been used once.

☑ **Inspect the sealant application around inspection hatches, through-hull fittings, screws or bolts.** Excessive amounts of sealant may indicate a poor fit or poorly drilled holes. Finishing touches
tell a lot. Poorly sealed fittings tend to leak.

☑ **Is there standing water in what are supposed to be dry storage areas?** If
there's water down there now, there always will be later.
Dry storage is precious on a small boat.

☑ **Look closely for watermarks around hatches and portholes, especially in
cabin models.** Watermarks indicate leaks, which will only get
worse. They are also a sign of poor fit and finish. Go find
another boat: there are plenty to choose from.

☑ **Is there standing water in the fish boxes and livewell?** This may indicate badly designed boxes or drains. If these don't drain
completely, they are a nuisance to keep clean and, in
general, suggest a poor design.

☑ **Check out the rubrail.** Is it smooth and even, or wavy and un-even? At the very least, a rubrail out of true indicates low quality or a poor job of attachment; at worst, a defective hull-to-deck joint. As you may recall from section 2 (page 7), the rubrail is where the hull and deck sections are fastened together on most boats. On such boats the rubrail is crucial to the structure and watertight integrity of the hull. Look carefully: a rubrail can hide a multitude of sins. If the hull and hull-liner unit did not fit correctly when mated, the builder may have used an excessive amount of sealant to fill in the gaps. In this case, the fasteners may be exerting pressure to hold the joint together. When the joint is stressed, as in a rough sea, cracks and splits may appear and leaks will follow when the sealant fails. Look below the rail. There should be a thin, even line of sealant. The more caulking I see, the less I like the boat.

☑ **Stand back and examine the whole picture.** Is there an uneven fit of deck to hull? Look at the bow from directly ahead. It should be perfectly symmetrical. Likewise from the stern. This may sound basic, but I've seen some remarkably mis-shapen hulls on new boats. I knew of a brand new $300,000 cruiser that took on several gallons of water through the hull-to-deck joint each time the boat hit a big wave. Even the best manufacturers goof up occasionally.

☑ **Inspect the vinyl and canvas.** There should be no dried-out, discolored, cracked, or torn vinyl or canvas on a new boat. If so, the boat may have been sitting out in the weather for a long time (and perhaps is a leftover), or inferior materials may have been used.

If after the inspection you feel this particular model suits you, get the brochure, thank the salesperson, and leave. Then call the manufacturer (the number will be in the brochure) with any questions you have. For the

final inspection and sea trial, we will want to be sure of
the maximum RPMs of the motor, the normal operating
temperature of the motor, what warning systems are standard (such as overheat, low oil, or low fuel), and how they
work. You might also want to ask about details of construction, warranties, and handling characteristics—
especially if you plan on taking the boat offshore.

The Negotiation Process

Now let's return to our salesperson. We'll follow a scenario that incorporates all of the most challenging circumstances. The salesperson, while likable, is tough. He
or she hasn't surrendered much at all. It's September, and
you have your eye on that newly arrived 19-foot center
console priced at $19,995 MSRP (note that all of the
figures we will use are imaginary and only for the purpose of illustration). The boat has a lot of options, some
of which you don't need. Let's go to work. If we can pull
this off, we can do anything!

This 19-footer is your first pick, but hopefully
you've selected two or three boats that are worth buying. I
like to target more than one boat because, once again, the
ability to walk away will save you thousands of dollars.
The dealer does not need to know his model is the one
your prefer, so we'll keep that just between us for now.

Once you've determined at home the *total* you
want to pay for the boat, return to the dealership with
your notes and look for your salesperson. Find him. Does
he call you by name? If not, he probably doesn't remember. That's good. He's not as sharp as you thought he was.
Tell him you're back for one last look before making your
purchasing decision. Does he remember the boat you were
interested in? Don't tell him: make him take you to it.

Ask him again, "What is your best cash price on this boat?" The strategy here is to determine how strongly their pricing structure is set. He should be able to answer you almost immediately. This markdown price should always be the same. If he needs to go and check his notes, you can bet that this price is flexible—and flexibility will always work in your favor. If he doesn't remember the figure he quoted you on your last visit (shame on him), look at your notes and remind him.

Tell him you came back to see if he still had the boat. You're glad it's not gone. You wanted one last look before making up your mind about which boat to buy. You liked a lot of things about the boat (name some if you want) and, although it may not be equipped exactly as you'd like, it will do nicely. Here we are telling the salesperson that while we have an interest, we are not convinced that this is the boat we'll end up buying. He needs to sweeten the deal by offering you more incentives to buy.

He'll no doubt ask about his competition. Play this down for now and concentrate on looking over the boat you intend to buy. Ask any pertinent questions he may not yet have answered. Make him resell you the boat. Have him remind you of the option list. This is not the time to get confused about who has a better boat that's equipped with what. You should already know which boat you prefer and why, and we'll assume this one is your first choice.

TIP

On your return trip to the dealership, ask the price again. If the salesperson needs to consult his notes, you can bet the price is flexible.

Ask him how much the boat would be without this option or that option. The strategy here is to establish the fact that you do not wish to pay for options already on this boat that you may not want or need. You are, in effect, removing the value of each of these options from the deal.

He will probably try to point out the benefits of these options, but you do not care because you do not value those benefits. If you're unhappy with parts of the layout, equipment, hardware, etc., now is the time to point this out politely. Do not make a big issue of it: just indicate what you like and what you dislike. Use the touch method described earlier to bring attention to any imperfections (see section 12 on inspecting a used boat, page 63). Do not agree or disagree with him when he tries to minimize these small imperfections. Just move on. You're impartially assessing his product, weighing the advantages and disadvantages carefully. Do not talk much; it's not necessary. Keep looking around. He'll be impressed with your thoroughness. When you've run out of ammunition, you have accomplished all you can on the lot. Go inside to his office.

Ask him, again, if they have any boats of that model arriving in the next few days. This expresses the fact that, while you like the model, this particular boat does not satisfy you completely. (His job is to attempt to sell you what he has on the lot first and, if all else fails, to order you in a new boat.) If he says yes, get all of the information. See if you can get a cash discount on that one.

Remember that ordering in a new boat may take 4 to 6 weeks, but at a savings of 4 to 8 percent. (August through October is the time period that brings the greatest savings; January through May brings the lowest.) In that fall period, you might save up to $1,000 on a $20,000 boat and get one equipped exactly as you like. But keep in mind that it's very difficult to get a dealer to pass that discount on to you. Raise the issue of a cash discount for ordering in a boat only when you cannot get the deal you want on a boat in stock. Go back another day and work that deal.

For this scenario, we'll assume that another model is not being delivered soon. Now, let's recap.

You've asked the salesperson for his best cash price. Worst case scenario here is that we remain at $1,000 under MSRP. If he's taken a firm stand, we've only reduced the $19,995 to around $18,995 (plus freight and prep, or F/P). The salesperson insists that this is the best he can do. Assuming only a 30 percent markup, his original invoice was about $15,380. Let's add that freight and prep for him. This boat costs $350 to ship and $250 to rig, for a total of $600. Our total cash price at this point is $18,995 plus $600, or $19,595.

The math you did before you left the house means you knew what you wanted to pay for the boat before you set foot in the boatyard: this is very important. In this scenario, we approximated our offer at $17,500 (the correct formula is $15,380 divided by 88 percent). Always assume you must add freight and prep charges to your totals. You are, for all intents and purposes, $1,500 apart. If you're timing this correctly, it's near the end of the month. Pressure is on your salesperson and the dealership to move another unit. He knows that you're shopping, that you're qualified to buy, and that this is your second or third visit. He's excited at the prospect of being so close to a sale. The remaining issue here is simple: is he willing to let you walk and lose a sale more than you're willing to walk and lose the boat? This all comes down to your determination and your mindset. The ability to walk away, in this case, will save you $1,500.

Tell him that you've been shopping and that there are other boats you're considering. They're not the same, but each appeals to you in its own way. You're out looking today for the absolute best deal you can make on one of them. It could very well be this one, but it's still too expensive. It has some options that you like but don't necessarily need. You'd rather not pay extra to have them. You have given the matter a great deal of thought, and you need to be at a price more like $17,500—not

$18,995. Ask him, "What do you think?" Then be quiet and wait. Don't be baited into a response if he says that this offer will not do. Be mentally prepared to walk.

Don't allow him to change your focus by talking monthly payment. You're not a payment buyer. You want his best bottom line, and nothing else will earn your business. Even if you would consider dealer financing, at this point you should keep the focus on the bottom line and not the monthly payment (for more on financing, see appendix 1, page 144).

He'll probably do a double take and jokingly state that he couldn't possibly "give" the boat away at that price. He may ask you if this is your best or final offer. Politely say yes. He may not commit. Instead, he may say that he might be able to get you a better price for an immediate cash deal and ask, "Are you ready to do business now?"

If you don't need a trade-in on your existing boat, tell him that if he can get you that boat for $17,500, you're ready to do business now. If you need to trade, see the discussion beginning on page 126.

He may still try to stand his ground and say that his boss will never take that kind of offer on a new boat. After all, it has only been on the lot for a month and it will take time to replace, if it sells. "I can probably get the boat price down to $18,500, but that would be rock bottom."

When he's done saying whatever else he feels he needs to add, do this. Pull out your checkbook and place it in front of you on his desk and simply say that you're ready to buy a boat today. "Why don't we ask your boss?" He'll have no choice but to present the offer to his boss. If he fool-

TRAP

Don't be distracted with talk about monthly payments. You're not a payment buyer. Focus on the best bottom line price.

ishly insists on not taking the offer to his boss, insist on talking to his boss yourself. (We will address the structure of the written offer in section 26. We are only concerned with the negotiation process here.)

You're a serious, prequalified buyer who has narrowed down his choices to the best three boats. You like each boat for different reasons and are prepared to buy one right now. If you leave this boatyard, chances are very good that you'll be buying Boat B or C down the road, today. You feel that this may be the best of the three boats and you would probably rather buy this one, but you're only budgeted for $17,500. You have gone so far as to show him that you're ready to write a check: you are buying today! If they cannot meet your needs now, you're going to have to go look at boat B; if they don't sell you that boat, you will go and buy boat C.

Notice that I've purposely left out freight and prep. This is your bargaining chip. Our figures for the purchase including F/P are $18,100. You have a $600 cushion at this point.

He is now in his manager's office wondering how things went so wrong. He presents your offer and tells his boss that you're ready to write a check now if we can make this deal. He'll tell the sales manager that he tried to get you at $18,500 with no luck. They will do some number crunching and determine that you are way low but not out of the ballpark.

The sales manager may talk to you personally, explaining that they cannot possibly sell you the boat for less than $18,500. He or she may consider a $100 or $200 courtesy discount for an immediate sale, then ask, "What do you think?"

This is why you need a clear plan going in. Define the total you will spend and stick with it. Don't turn control of the situation over to them. Never talk payments; always talk bottom line. You're the consumer, the one wanting to spend your hard-earned cash. Consider how long it takes and how much work is required for you to earn $20,000. Don't part with your money lightly.

Tell him (nicely) that, as soon as you leave here, you're going out to buy a boat today at another dealer if you cannot buy the boat here. You need to stay in your budget; it's as simple as that. You want to buy a boat today, and you're sure that you'll be able to find a boat that will suit your needs. You've already looked. They each have one that appeals to you. You'd rather have this boat, but all you want to spend is $17,500.

They'll probably try to point out the superiority of their boat. Let them talk and don't say a word. Tell them (when they are through) that you realize this and that is why you came here first. But you're sticking to your budget. "I'm ready to write you a deposit check now. What do you think?"

They will have to leave and talk. If they do, you've done well. The sales manager will probably ask the salesperson if he thinks you'd be willing to pay for freight and prep. If and when he asks that question, you've won!

When he returns and asks you if you'd be willing to pay freight and prep, ask how much? He may try to add on some more profit here, so be careful. Stick to your original figure. Tell him you had allotted $600 to cover this expense, and that's it. You still have to cover sales taxes and registration. Make him compromise down to your figure. He was probably expecting outright rejection, so your $600 limit will be acceptable. Who knows: you may not even get bumped for the freight and prep.

What about That Trade?

Trade-in deals are arrived at using the cash value of your trade (minus any amount owed), plus the balance of actual cash it will take to equal the best bottom line. This is referred to simply as the difference. If you need to throw in the trade, here's how.

Make it his idea. Tell him you're prepared to buy as soon as your boat sells. He'll probably ask you if you've had any bites. Tell him whatever the truth is. For our purposes, let's say, no. Next he will ask you the amount for which you're trying to sell it. Tell him you're using the highest figure (plus options) that he quoted you last time you were here. Show him his card with the numbers written on the back.

He'll probably try to find a way to work in the trade. If he asks you if you'd be interested in trading, say yes—as long as you get a fair deal. He'll be quick to throw in that he will not be able to give you the higher figure listed on the card and still discount his boat. Tell him to do his best and turn him loose. Many times the salesperson will bring his boat back up to retail ($19,995) and bring you back a paper (and an awkward explanation) showing you a high value on your boat against his: sort of retail for retail. All we are interested in is the difference.

Here goes. Your boat is worth either $5,500 high (trade) or $4,000 low (trade). Retail will undoubtedly be higher. His boat is worth $19,995 high and (by your figures) $17,500 low. Your target difference is the $17,500 minus $4,000, or $13,500 (plus F/P).

He'll probably come back with his at $19,995 minus yours at $5,500, or a difference of $14,495. Looks like we are about $1,000 apart. Of course, at this point he has yet to see your boat. You can still write the deal subject to his inspection of your boat.

Tell him he's close, but if you were to trade in your boat, you would want to be out of pocket no more than $13,500. That would be giving him $19,000 for his boat if he will give you $5,500 for yours, and you feel that is a fair trade. You like his boat, but it has some options that you don't need. You had intended on waiting until you could sell your boat, so that you could get the best cash price and don't want to lose money by trading it in. He has given you a good idea, and you will go and see what kind of offers you can get from the dealers for boats B and C.

Tell him that if he can get you the boat for a $13,500 difference, you will do business with him, right now. Make him present this to the sales manager. Here is what they've got.

Their boat cost them $15,380. By taking your offer of $13,500 (plus your boat) they will have $1,880 into your boat. Assuming it sells down the road for $5,500, they are making $3,620 total profit on both deals. That's $1,500 more than your cash offer would have netted them.

This is a tough decision on their part. If they come back with only the freight and prep added on, you've won! If they try to split the difference, plus F/P, you must hold firm. A dealer will generally try to take a trade at 20 percent below low book value. The values are there. They may give you 50 reasons why it will not work, but the bottom line is they must earn your business. Stick to the difference figure you had in mind. Tell them you're willing to go an additional $600 for the freight and prep, but that's all you have in your budget. Tell them you must see about getting a better deal down the road or wait until you sell the boat. If they won't consider your offer, you must walk and work the next dealer.

Ordering a New Boat

We've gotten down here because we cannot get the deal we want on a boat in stock. They have refused our offer or our trade or both. Call them back. Talk to your salesperson. Ask him if the dealership gets a discount for ordering in a new boat to be paid for in cash when it arrives. Ninety-nine times out of a hundred you'll get an immediate yes. Tell him that if he can put the deal to-

TIP

Ordering a custom boat from the factory should cost you less, not more.

gether on the same boat special ordered you'll do business with him today. Let him call you back.

Let's go back to the trade-in deal. We're $1,000 apart. The cost of the boat was $15,380. With a discount of even only 4 percent (it's September), his cost will be $14,788. Now we are only $408 apart. He'll take that deal anytime. You'll probably have to give him your boat or a strong deposit to order it in.

On a straight cash deal, you may approach him a bit differently. Ask him to tell you what kind of discount he gets for a cash deal. He may try to hold back. That's OK, but make him tell you something. If he tells you 4 percent, for example, figure out that discount and split the difference with him on the deal. So if he wouldn't go for $17,500 for the boat on site and is claiming to get a $587 discount (4 percent), tell him you'll do business right now for $17,200 (that is the $17,500 minus $300, or approximately half of $587). Explain that they won't have to do anything but order the boat and deliver it to you. They won't be out of stock by selling you the one on the lot; they won't have to pay someone to maintain it on the lot. It will go right to you. It will make them look great to the manufacturer. They'll be getting you for a service customer. You'll tell all of your friends to buy here. They'll take the deal in a heartbeat.

Leftovers

With a lot of calls and a little luck, you may be able to find a new model from last year still on a dealer's lot. These are very desirable at the right price. You must learn to read between the lines, however, and not be fooled by markdowns and sales.

For example, if the new model is $19,995 MSRP and the older model is on sale for $18,995, you can probably do better negotiating on the newer one first. The new-boat invoice cost is around $15,380 (excluding freight and prep). A 15 percent deal on the new one is about $18,100. Now let's assume that the invoice cost on last year's boat was 5 percent less (prices rise about 5 percent a year on average), or $14,811. At a 15 percent markup, the bottom-line sale last year should have been $17,425! For a $675 difference, I'd take the new one any day.

Remember that the dealer needs to move that leftover. He is in all likelihood paying $130 a month while it sits on the lot. A solid offer of no higher than $16,100 is called for here and may well take it. That is a little less than 9 percent over invoice (remember, you must add freight and prep).

Warranties

Warranties are one of the strongest arguments for buying a new rather than a used boat. Every manufacturer warrants his new product one way or another. On a new-boat purchase, you'll be receiving several different warranties, including hull, motor, and trailer.

TIP

If you can afford it, buy an extended warranty for the whole boat—or at least for the engine.

I will state here that warranties are valuable when still in force and transferable at the time of resale. They have tangible monetary value. If you can afford one at the time of purchase, I recommend getting an extended warranty package from a reputable company. If you don't get one on the whole boat, at least get one on the engine.

Hull Warranty

I've seen hull warranties extend from as little as 90 days to a lifetime. At present the industry standard is 5 years. It's a good idea to actually read a printed warranty, available from the manufacturer, before purchase.

First off, not many hull warranties are transferable. They apply only to the original purchaser. Second, they usually cover electrical and mechanical systems only for the first year. Many of the individual components have their own warranties, such as the bilge pump or the stereo. The boat manufacturer often will replace the unit in question and deal with the part manufacturer directly; the manufacturer may cover labor charges for removal and installation. Ask a manufacturer's representative about component coverage if you get a chance; if not, ask the dealership sales manager. Finally, the very long-term warranties get hazy in the later years. You may end up paying the lion's share of a repair down the road. These are called conditional or limited warranties.

TIP

Hull warranties are not unconditional: read *all* the fine print carefully.

As I've mentioned, the stability of the company that manufactures your boat is a huge factor. If the builder disappears tomorrow, who will honor your warranty? Even some of the better builders experience financial problems from time to time. Your best bet is both a manufacturer and a dealer with a good track record.

Motor Warranty

Most motor warranties cover only the first year, although some go up to three years. If you study the longer warranties, you'll find lots of fine print, especially after the first year. Most require that the motor be handled only by

factory-authorized personnel. In addition, they may ask
for your maintenance records in the event of a major warranty claim, so be sure to keep those up to date. This is
where extended warranties do the most good. Even smaller
motor repairs can be quite costly. An extended warranty
can protect your entire engine for up to six years. They are
almost always transferable, with a small transfer fee and are
honored nationwide. You generally do not have to purchase these right away, although many salespeople would
lead you to believe that you do (they make money on the
sale of these, too). You should be able to wait almost until
your first year of original warranty expires.

Trailer Warranty

These are usually good for about two years. It's good to establish right off who will be handling these warranty repairs. Is the boat dealership equipped to do so? Will the
trailer have to be returned to the factory? (And just exactly
where is that?) How will you do any boating in the mean-
time? The answers to these and all the rest of your pertinent questions are usually just a phone call away, directly to
the manufacturer. (I've been in sales for over eleven years
and still could not answer these questions without a few
calls.) Tires, couplers, brakes, bearings, axles, and springs
may all have different warranties, so pay attention here.

The Buyer's Order

Now that we have all of that ugliness out of the way (I
shouldn't say ugliness, since we never need to stoop to
lies and deceit), we are going to sort all of this out on
paper. The dealership will have a standard contract form,
with lots and lots of fine print on the back side to pro-

tect their interests. Read it well: this is $20,000 you're throwing around here. The front, however, should be fairly straightforward. Much of it will be filled in by your salesperson by hand. Make sure it contains the following.

- ▣ your full name, address, and phone number

- ▣ their name, address, and phone number

- ▣ the date

- ▣ date of delivery and any pertinent instructions

- ▣ the manufacturer, model, year, and hull identification number of the boat

- ▣ the manufacturer, model, year and serial number of the motor or motors

- ▣ the manufacturer, model, year, and serial number of the trailer

- ▣ a box next to each, clearly marked, indicating each is new and not used

- ▣ a listing of all options both already on the boat and those to be added (you'll want very exacting descriptions of the latter)

- ▣ a full description of your trade-in and the amount of cash value given for it

- ▣ a full accounting of all monetary charges. Compare the bottom line before taxes. Check that addition. Anyone can make an honest mistake.

If the dealer adds a service fee that seems excessive, object now. Often a dealer will try to build in some additional profit here as service, office, or yard fees. Not one dealer in a hundred will blow the deal over these fees. Be firm and don't pay an excess.

If you buy a used boat from an individual, you're responsible for paying sales tax (proof of payment is required to register the boat). When you buy from a dealership, the dealer is responsible for collecting sales tax. In some states, the dealer actually registers the boat for you. In that case, it's customary for you to pay for registration, but the fee shouldn't be over (or much over) $100. One call to the tax collector's office will verify the registration costs.

Your contract or buyer's order needs to contain this information at a minimum. Now for the contingencies.

☐ **The entire deposit is refundable to the buyer.** Some dealers may try to keep your deposit if the deal goes south for any reason. It may even be in the small print on the back somewhere. I recently had a customer commit to purchasing a boat from my dealership. Because he was still shopping, he put a bid on a boat at another dealership as a backup. They were fully aware that he had signed a contract with my dealership, and assured him that his deposit was fully refundable. Alas, he purchased my boat, returned to the other dealership for his deposit, and was refused! The victim of an unscrupulous dealer and the fine print. (Despite what they promised, a no-refund provision was buried in the contract.) In the end all he did was file a complaint against the dealer with the Better Business Bureau, and he was not the first to do so. If you find yourself in this situation, small claims court is an option, although in my experience this avenue is less promising against a dealer with a standard contract than it is with a private seller who is withholding your deposit. In the case I've just described, an initial inquiry to the Better Business Bureau could have saved my client some grief. Overall, the best way to protect yourself is to read the fine print, have them strike out offending clauses (such cross-outs must be initialed by all parties), and get all promises in writing.

On the other hand, a dealership should have the right to keep a deposit if it has suffered financially by taking a boat off the market for an extended period and the buyer subsequently backed out of the deal. To protect both parties, every contract should specify in writing a reasonable and definite time period during which the deposit is refundable.

▣ **This sale is subject to satisfactory financing.** (Don't spell out rates and terms here.) If you cannot get the rate and terms promised or expected, you're not obligated to complete the deal and your deposit is refunded to you.

▣ **This sale is subject to satisfactory sea trial.** Don't elaborate here either. If for any reason during the sea trial you find that the boat is not right for you, you're not obligated to complete the deal and your deposit is refunded to you.

▣ **This sale is subject to satisfactory mechanical inspection.** On a used-boat purchase from a dealership, keep this option open. If your mechanic says no, you're not obligated to complete the deal and your deposit is refunded to you.

I'm not an attorney and wouldn't presume to tell you what is or is not the correct wording for each of these phrases in your area. As with all contracts of this magnitude, if in doubt you may want to consult an attorney for proper legal advice.

If and when you are completely satisfied, sign and date it where indicated. Next, an officer of the corporation—an owner or an authorized sales manger—must sign and date this agreement for it to be binding. Be sure to get a complete, original carbon copy of the buyer's order to take with you.

The Final Inspection

Should you do a final inspection on a new boat? Most certainly. At this point, you're ready to take the boat out on sea trial. The following is largely a reprint of the sea trial checklist for buying a used boat, as the criteria for the sea trial are essentially the same.

Help the salesperson drop the boat in the water. If you're new at this, he may have some good advice for you here. Be observant of all that he does. Once launched, check out the following.

☑ **Does the boat float level when empty?** It may sound silly, but if the boat lists at the dock, it will list underway and be harder to handle. An inherent list could be due to poor design or weight distribution.

☑ **Observe the start-up procedure.**

☑ **Are all the gauges functioning properly?**

☑ **Are all the warning buzzers working?** Some newer boats have low oil, low fuel, and overheat warning systems; you'll typically hear a chirp when the key is first turned. This is one of the points we called the manufacturer to check about in the checklist for a new-boat inspection. Water may be circulating, but not properly. The motor could be running hot without any obvious signs. If there is no temperature gauge or the overheat warning system is inoperative, you may never know a problem exists.

☑ **Do all the lights work?**

☑ **Are all the electronics working?**

☑ **Once again, test bilge pump (this allows you to find the pump and look to see if the boat takes on any water).**

☑ **Does the starter sound strong?** Does it crank without hesitation?

☑ **Examine all the fuel lines you can for leaks while the engine is running.**

Now take the boat out.

☑ **Does the boat idle okay under load (in gear)?**

☑ **Does the engine perform well at all speeds?**

☑ **Will the engine rev up to the proper maximum RPM?** (You should have checked this value with the manufacturer.)

☑ **Take the helm.** Does the boat steer easily?

☑ **Tilt the motor up partway.** Does it remain there under load?

☑ **How does the boat handle a following sea?** Is it really wet? If this is a big factor, talk about this with the salesperson. You have not yet purchased the boat. If you intend on going deep sea fishing and diving, this is a critical factor and may make you decide against the purchase.

☑ **Warn everyone and take the boat from three-quarter throttle to idle very quickly.** Look back. Does the boat take on water over the transom?

☑ **Shift into reverse gear.** Slowly bring up the throttle. Are you taking on water over the transom?

☑ **How's the water circulation in the motor?** All outboards should shoot out a telltale stream of water (a "pisser," for lack of a more delicate word). This should be a steady jet of water even at idle. An inboard/outboard or inboard should always have a working temperature gauge and as a rule not exceed about 180°F. This is another value to confirm with the manufacturer.

☑ **Does the charging system work?** A normal reading on the gauge should be 13 to 14 volts.

Take your time and enjoy the ride. Your salesperson should be taking this time to show you how all of the systems operate and to explain the break-in procedures. Additionally, this is a good time to go over that list of options on the buyer's order and check to see that they are properly installed and in good working order. When

Take Your Time: Check Everything

I recently sold a brand new, 20-foot center console to a local fireman. In the rush to get the boat delivered on time, I personally took off the aluminum prop, went inside, and grabbed the stainless steel prop my parts department had special-ordered for him. I quickly installed it and he picked up the boat. On his first day out, he called and told me that when he throttled in reverse to get the boat off the trailer, it lurched forward. The supplier, it turned out, had sent a left-handed prop by mistake. This sort of ruined his first outing, I'd say. I apologized profusely, re-ordered the proper stainless prop, and donated the aluminum prop for good measure. Everybody makes mistakes, so take your time and check everything.

you have decided that you're comfortable, knowledgeable, and happy, take the boat back in.

Upon your return to the dealership, take a moment to verify all three identification numbers: boat, motor, and trailer.

Start at the rear of the hull. The hull identification number is located on the stern, usually on the starboard (right) side, just under the rubrail. Next, the motor serial number (outboard) should be stamped on a small plate fastened to the motor bracket. It can be on the left or right side, depending on the manufacturer. On an in-board/outboard or inboard, the serial number is generally stamped on the top of the engine. The trailer number is sometimes stamped right into the framework, but it's usually on a tag. Either way, it will be located up front, within 2 or 3 feet of the "wishbone" of the frame. When in doubt, ask your salesperson to show you.

Next, you'll want to take a final look around. Once again, start at the stern and slowly walk all of the way around the boat and look for chips, cracks, dents, scratches, etc. This is your new boat. It should be perfect! Next get back up inside and do the same. Check out all of the hardware; it should be straight and tight. Look over all of the canvas and vinyl. Be thorough. Only when you're totally satisfied should you proceed to go inside and close the deal. Remember, if the dealership isn't taking care of you now, they never will.

The Purchase

Prior to your arrival at the dealership to close the deal, you will need to visit your banker and procure a cashier's check or bank draft for the entire amount due, as listed on the buyer's order.

If you're financing, you will be spending a little time at your lending institution. They will have a series of papers for you to sign. We will be covering these details in appendix 1, "Financing 101" (see page 144). You'll probably end up bringing a bank draft to the dealership. Most of the ones I've seen are printed on the side of an envelope. Whatever it may look like, this represents a great deal of cash, so hang on and take good care of it.

If the dealership is taking care of the financing for you, be cautious. They'll be printing up the financial contract. I have seen unscrupulous types who attempt to add higher interest, insurance you'd rather not have, and even the additional cost of the extended warranty in an effort

TRAP

Read financial contracts carefully to be sure the dealership doesn't slip in additional profit.

to sell you more and raise their profit. Most dealerships are fair and reputable, but always err on the side of caution. Read that financial contract carefully. Don't be rushed. Some states impose additional taxes and filing fees. These are modest amounts (usually not more than $100) and are normal and unavoidable.

You'll now sit down with your

salesperson to conclude the financial part of the deal. He should have in his possession the original copy of the buyer's order. Borrow it from him and verify that it matches yours exactly, with no unauthorized additions or subtractions. Any agreed upon changes should be initialed by all concerned parties.

At this point you should receive all information booklets associated with your purchase. Included here should be all your written warranties, a boat owner's manual, an owner's manual for the motor and trailer, and manuals on all the electronics. You should receive a temporary registration (in some states, the buyer's order marked "Paid in Full" will do) and a temporary tag for the trailer. Be as thorough as possible and examine your paperwork to be sure no information booklets or warranties were overlooked.

When you're satisfied that all is in order, turn over the draft or cashier's check and have the original buyer's order stamped "Paid in Full," initialed, and turned over to you. Congratulations!

Ask your salesperson who will be filing the warranties on the boat, motor, and trailer. They may take responsibility for one or all three. I like to have this all clarified up front. Generally, you will file the warranty information on the individual electronics and other systems.

Maintenance Tips

This is a brand new piece of equipment. Treat it well and maintain it correctly, and it will give you many years of service. All motors have a specific regimen for their break-in period. Consult your dealer's service manager for details and follow them religiously.

Before Each Use

☑ Install the bilge drain plug.

☑ Verify that the battery has a good charge.

☑ Inspect all of your safety gear.

☑ Inspect the electronics; make sure they power up.

☑ Inspect for any leaks. This includes engine gas or oil, hydraulic fluid from steering or trim tabs, water from livewells or in bilge, and so forth.

☑ Open up the bilge area and aerate lower levels.

☑ Run the bilge pump to make sure it's working properly.

☑ Stow all gear properly.

☑ Visually inspect the motor.

After Each Use

☑ After use in salt water, flush the motor.

☑ Hose all dirt and salt from the boat, motor, and trailer.

☑ Clean the inside of the boat thoroughly.

☑ Remove the bilge drain plug (but not, of course, if you leave it in a wet slip).

☑ Examine the propeller for damage.

☑ Turn the battery switch to the off position.

Monthly or Bimonthly

☑ Spray down the engine block with a silicone-based spray to prevent corrosion. Try to keep it away from the carburetor intakes.

☑ Grease all grease points on the motor and trailer (gimble bearings on an inboard/outboard).

☑ Polish and protect all stainless steel fittings and rails.

☑ Treat the vinyl with a preservative.

☑ Treat canvas with a preservative.

☑ Spray exposed electrical connections with electrical contact cleaner.

☑ Check the lower unit gearcase oil.

☑ Lubricate hinges and canvas snaps.

☑ Check belts and hoses (inboard/outboard and inboard).

☑ Check battery fluid level or levels.

☑ Check all lighting for bad bulbs, connections, etc.

☑ Check through-hull fittings for a proper seal. Check gate valves for proper operation.

☑ Check drain hoses and clamps.

100-Hour Service

A hundred hours is considered to be equivalent to one year of use.

☑ Tune the engine.

☑ Change the lower unit oil.

☑ Change fuel/water separator.

☑ Replace water pump impeller.

☑ Replace zincs.

Examine the following.

☑ hoses and belts

- ☑ fuel system

- ☑ warning systems

- ☑ oil pump

- ☑ trim/tilt unit

- ☑ steering system

- ☑ throttle system

- ☑ electrical wiring and connections

- ☑ screws, nuts, and bolts (for tightness)

- ☑ bilge pump operation

- ☑ blower operation

- ☑ gauges

- ☑ all safety gear

- ☑ all lines

There are many other day-to-day or month-to-month duties to observe. The more complex your setup, the more you need to do. If you have air-conditioning, a generator, trim tabs, a raw-water strainer, a holding tank, a freshwater tank, a portable marine head, electronics, an automatic fire-extinguishing system, an inverter, dual batteries, and so on, these will need attention, too. Ask your dockmaster, salesperson, mechanic, or boating friend how to maintain your individual systems. Don't worry: by nature, boaters are the type of people who'll give you all the advice you'll ever need, and then some.

Remember, there is honesty, integrity, and truth in the vast majority of people out there. But for the rest, "Let the seller beware!"

Appendix

Financing 101

You can easily finance even older boats. Marine lenders are not as restrained as automobile lenders, and there are plenty of marine lenders out there. These lenders use the *N.A.D.A. Appraisal Guide* and other pricing guides described in section 7 on pricing (see page 48) to determine a boat's current value, and they will generally lend up to 75 percent of market value. They'll usually offer terms of at least two years on older boats, and four to six years is not uncommon. Remember, they are rating you as much as they're rating the vessel.

On new boats, most lenders base estimated value on the invoice cost plus 35 percent. Depending on your credit history, they may lend up to 100 percent of the sale price if they are shown significant equity (difference) between the purchase price and the MSRP (in our previous example, $16,995 versus $19,995). We have a good shot at that in our purchase scenario: we are showing at least $3,000 equity. Most lenders will give you their best rate only when you give them a minimum of 10 percent down in cash. It's also worth noting that boat lenders will not excuse a poor credit history as easily as a car lender can. Their reasoning here is that if you get into financial straits, the toys will be the first to go unpaid.

You can usually be preapproved by your regular bank for a particular amount of money, even though you have not yet chosen a boat. This is a powerful bargaining tool. To the owner or salesperson, preapproval seems just like a handful of cash. You will be able to cut

TIP

If you get a good deal (purchase price much lower than MSRP), the lender may lend up to 100 percent of the sale price.

right to the bottom line for a new boat, and a boatowner will be more likely to drop his price if he knows that you are serious enough about buying to have already taken this step.

If you go through a dealer, they probably have several excellent sources at their disposal. Others advertise regularly in boating magazines and even the trader magazines. When considering dealer financing, keep this in mind: They sell financing for profit, just as they sell boats for profit. There are many factors to consider when shopping for financing. Rate and term are the most important. This is how it works.

The interest rate is based on the amount borrowed, and it goes *down* as the amount goes up. A lender may charge 9.5 percent for a $10,000 loan, yet lend the same person $15,000 at 9.25 percent. This is a graduated scale, with divisions at $10,000, $15,000, $25,000, $50,000, and $100,000. The graduation is usually a quarter point per division. The interest rate itself will fluctuate as any other, but the dollar value cutoffs are effectively fixed and the quarter-point graduation is typical. For examples, see the table on graduated interest rates.

Graduated Interest Rates	
Lending Amount	Rate
Up to $10,000	9.99%
$10,001 to $15,000	9.75%
$15,001 to $25,000	9.50%
$25,001 to $50,000	9.25%
$50,001 to 100,000	8.99%

Now comes the sales part. A dealer (or a bank, for that matter) will attempt to get the best interest rate from you that they can. Let's assume the interest rates listed above represent the "buy rates"—the rates at which a retail lender can obtain financing. Based on our table, you will be quoted 11.75 percent on a $15,000 loan, which nets the lender 2 percent over his buy rate and substantial profits over the term of the loan. This increase may represent only a $17 increase in monthly payments, from $196 to $213, based on a ten-year term. Chances are the average consumer will accept this.

And this is what they count on. They will, no doubt, attempt to justify this in some way or another, but what it comes down to is sales technique. You'll be told that the more you borrow, the higher the interest rate. Your credit is good, but not perfect. That late payment you made in 1972 really hurt you. The longer you borrow, the greater the risk, so they must charge you a higher interest rate. You are close to being maxed out on your credit limit, so the risk is greater and so is the interest rate. The psychology behind the sale is that you are now so psyched about the purchase that the interest rate is arbitrary. It isn't.

You know your credit situation better than anyone. If you're close to being maxed out, then a slight increase in interest may be in order, but not 2 percentage points. Lenders today are very competitive and it pays to shop. What you need to keep in mind is that

TIP

The more you must borrow, the lower the interest should be.

one financing offer is not the final word on the matter. A loan can be overpriced just as a boat can be overpriced. Tell them that you feel the interest rate is not satisfactory, and you will have to shop it around. Name a reasonable interest rate and stick with it. Do not accept a longer term to

TRAP

Don't even consider a loan that penalizes you for early payment.

lower your payments. Stick to your guns and get the best rate or walk.

The dealerships are naturally in on it. The lender will pay a dealer as much as 1 percent of the value of the loan per quarter interest point. Sounds complicated, but it's worth exploring so stay with me. Let's keep the same figures. On a loan of $15,000 at 11.75 percent they have your loan at a full 2 percent over the buy rate (9.75 percent according to our chart). That dealership will be paid as follows.

$$\$15,000 \text{ X } 0.01 \text{ } (1\%) = \$150.00 \text{ X } 8 = \$1,200.00$$
of your hard earned money

We multiply by 8 because a 2 percent increase over the buy rate equals 8 quarter-points at 1 percent per quarter point. Suddenly that great deal you worked so hard to find isn't so great as it seemed.

Most lenders will also want to sell you insurance on your loan. It is called credit–life insurance. Should you become injured, the credit insurance will protect your credit by making your payments for you. Life insurance will pay off the loan should you die. If you want credit–life insurance, buy it. It is never required. If they insist on it when you don't want it, shop elsewhere.

In addition, consumer loans should be simple in-terest with no prepayment penalty. Most of them are, but some second-rate lenders will try to include a clause in with the loan that penalizes you for paying off the loan early. Don't even consider it. If they won't drop the pre-payment penalty clause, drop them.

I avoid variable interest loans. You gain a slightly lower initial interest rate, but it's something of a gamble

Insider's Guide to Buying a Powerboat

Typical Terms of Marine Loans	
Up to $10,000	7 years
$10,001 to $15,000	10 years
$15,001 to $25,000	12 years
$25,001 to $50,000	15 years
$50,000 on up	20 years

because the lender can periodically adjust the interest rate, usually every two years. They tie it to a T-bill index or some other indicator of the cost of money. Regardless of the index, the rate always seems to go up more than it goes down.

The next question is the term, or length, of the loan. Like the interest structure, term is based on the loan amount (this applies mainly to new boats). See the table above on typical loan terms for a realistic schedule.

Older boats fall into the two- to six-year category and the division points are not well defined. I think the lender just rolls the dice.

Remember that your loan depends mostly on you and your track record. If you have taken good care with your credit, you will be rewarded (albeit with a little negotiation) with lower interest rates and lower payments.

Use the Loan Payment Multiplier table, page 151, to help you get the jump on those wizards of lending. It is extremely accurate.

Enter the chart with your loan amount and multiply by the factor listed under your target term and rate; then divide by 1,000 for your payment. In our example above, the loan was $15,000 at 9.75 percent interest over ten years. Our answer: $196.20.

This chart is set up primarily for new boats. Al-

Insurance

Although a full treatment of boat insurance is beyond the scope of this book, the subject of financing leads directly to insurance. If you are financing the purchase of a boat and using the boat itself as collateral, the lender will almost always require that you carry insurance. That way, the balance of your loan will be covered if the boat is seriously damaged or lost.

A standard boat policy consists of hull coverage and liability coverage, which are roughly comparable to comprehensive-collision and liability coverage on a car. Of course, even if your boat is not financed, you should seriously consider insurance. In the area of liability, the analogy between boats and cars does not hold: you're not required by law to carry liability insurance on a boat, although the possibility always exists that you'll be held liable in an accident. Would you forego liability insurance on your car if the law did not require it?

Hull coverage provides for the repair or replacement of the boat if it is damaged or destroyed. Most boat insurance policies will cover the loss of the boat in any circumstance except those explicitly excluded. Typical exclusions include loss due to illegal use, defects in manufacture, or a lack of proper maintenance.

Insurance policies are further divided into *boat* policies and *yacht* policies. Although the line between them isn't sharply drawn, boat policies tend to cover smaller boats, such as open boats with outboards. Yacht policies cover more substantial and valuable boats. Nonetheless, many owners of small powerboats opt for a yacht policy.

A yacht policy will cover an absolute value for the boat agreed upon when the policy is issued; if a boat insured for $30,000 is a complete loss, your check should be for $30,000. You may be forced to lower the stated value of the boat over time in response to periodic surveys required by the insurer (every 5 years is typical), but until then the coverage amount is stable. Many boat policies, on the other hand, will reimburse you only for the current, depreciated value of the boat at the time of loss, as determined by a pricing guide such as those discussed in section 7 on pricing (see page 48). This may be significantly less than what you stated when the policy was drawn up. Not surprisingly, yacht polices tend to be more expensive.

(continued on page 150)

Be sure to inquire about depreciation when considering a policy. With both boat and yacht policies, you may be reimbursed for individual equipment items, such as canvas or propellers, at their depreciated value.

Some people insure their boats through a rider on their homeowner policy. As a rule you can only cover boats up to a certain size by this route, and the liability coverage conferred will not be as comprehensive as it is with a specialized policy.

The second component of a boat insurance policy is protection and indemnity coverage, which protects you from liability if you are involved in an accident and successfully sued. Unless it can be shown that you violated the terms of your policy, the insurance company will provide you with legal representation and cover any damages awarded against you up to the limit stated in the policy ($300,000 is a common value). It will also cover medical expenses up to a specified point. Of course, if damages exceed the limit in the policy, you are responsible for the difference.

As with car insurance, your demographic profile, background, and planned activities will affect the cost of coverage. A recent history of insurance claims will probably increase your premiums. If a high-speed powerboat is in question, a bad boating record—and sometimes even a bad driving record—will hurt you. Completion of a U.S. Power Squadrons or Coast Guard Auxiliary course in seamanship or piloting will help your premiums. Likewise, carrying more than the minimum required safety equipment should work in your favor.

Rates may be lower for boats that cruise in regions that are statistically less hazardous. In colder climates seasonal limitations are common: you'll pay less for the months the boat is out of the water, although if you put the boat in early you're violating the terms of the policy and won't be covered.

Finally, unlike automotive policies, boat policies cover activity within a defined geographical area. If you own a larger cruiser and plan an extended trip that'll take you out of your coverage area, inquire with your agent about an extension.

ways feel out the lender on older boats. You will usually
incur some other charges, such as minor taxes and fees,
as with most consumer loans. You may choose to pay
cash for those so they don't affect your payment amount.
Not all lenders pay out to dealerships. The bottom line is
always interest rate and term.

Loan Payment Multiplier

Term (years) Rate	10	12	15	20
6.99	11.61	10.28	8.98	7.75
7.25	11.74	10.42	9.12	7.90
7.50	11.88	10.56	9.28	8.06
7.75	12.01	10.69	9.42	8.21
7.99	12.14	10.83	9.56	8.37
8.25	12.27	10.97	9.71	8.53
8.50	12.40	11.11	9.85	8.68
8.75	12.54	11.24	10.00	8.84
8.99	12.67	11.39	10.15	9.00
9.25	12.81	11.53	10.30	9.16
9.50	12.94	11.67	10.45	9.33
9.75	13.08	11.81	10.60	9.49
9.99	13.22	11.96	10.75	9.66
10.25	13.36	12.10	10.90	9.82
10.50	13.50	12.25	11.06	9.99
10.75	13.64	12.39	11.21	10.16
10.99	13.78	12.54	11.37	10.33

Appendix

Author's Picks

It would be presumptuous and misleading for me to pretend to be an expert on every type of boat on the market today. The bulk of my sales experience has been in Florida, where I have specialized in center consoles, flats boats, walkaround cuddies, bowriders, and small cruisers. My experience with jet boats, personal watercraft, bass boats, pontoon boats, deckboats, larger cruisers, performance/ski boats, and cats is limited. With that caveat, let us proceed.

There are premium builders out there that consistently offer superior products at premium prices, as well as those that build good products for reasonable prices. I have listed the premium boat companies and the types of boats they build first. They are wonderful boats that hold their value well, but you pay for the brand. Then, I have followed with the quality builders and the boats they produce—boats that will give you similar service for less money.

Always remember that an older boat calls for careful inspection even if it was made by a premium builder.

Premium Boat Lines

Boston Whaler

Built in Edgewater, Florida. Center consoles, walk-around cuddies, dual consoles, and jet boats. The unsinkable reputation of this boatbuilder is eons old and well deserved. Even their smallest center consoles are stable and safe and are great first boats for kids. These boats are well built, but they tend to ride a bit rough and lack some of the more popular fishing amenities. But have faith. As of this writing they are changing their ways to better accommodate the serious anglers.

I like their smaller center consoles best (under 20 feet). The 15-foot Dauntless, 17-foot Montauk, and 19-foot/22-foot Outrage all have great resale value. About the only walk-around I've had any luck with is the 22-foot Revenge. Their little center console jet boat (Whaler Rage) is quite possibly the only jet boat I'd consider buying. Whalers command excellent resale value.

Contender

Built in Homestead, Florida. Center consoles and walk-around cuddies. Without a doubt, these are some of the best riding fishing boats out there. From the 21-foot center console to the 33-foot cuddy, these boats feature deep V hulls, superior construction quality, an exceptional ride, and a great fishing layout, even if they're somewhat spartan in amenities. These are not the fastest hulls out there, but I'd rather be in one of these when that squall line catches you 20 miles out. My personal preference are the 21-, 23-, 25-, and 27-foot center consoles. No bargains here, but you'll get your money back in resale.

Fountain

Built in Washington, North Carolina. Performance cuddies/cruisers, center consoles, and walk-around cuddies. In the world of offshore racing hulls, Reggie rules. A top quality builder, Fountain practically wrote the book on high performance monohulls with inboard/outboard power. If you want to go fast, get a lot of money and put it right here. The 28-footer is a great size as long as you don't need a big cabin. Layouts are predictable both inside and out. But that's not why you want one of these, is it?

Grady White

Built in Greenville, North Carolina. Center consoles, walk-around cuddies, dual consoles, and catamarans. Grady White makes the "mack daddy" (to quote my niece) of walk-arounds. Nice cabins, nicer seating, and well-thought-out layouts. They are also serious contenders in the center console (the smaller the better) and dual console categories (with two models, three counting the old 17-foot version).

The ride generally leaves a bit to be desired, but they are working on it. The 1999 26-foot cat hull and the 1999 31-foot center console are both awesome. Even older models hold up in quality and resale value. I prefer their cuddies in the mid-20-foot size range. They are quite popular, at least around Florida, as are the 20-foot Overnighter (small), 23-foot Gulfstream, 25-foot Sailfish, and the 28-foot Marlin.

Mako

Built in Miami, Florida. Center consoles, walk-around cuddies, dual consoles, and flats boats. Mako is the benchmark for affordable (barely) great riding center consoles and walk-arounds. Even their early 1970s hulls still command good money (inspect them carefully, as with any older hull). The later the model, the better equipped it will be for the serious angler. Earlier walk-arounds tend to be narrow, but they are very fast. I like anything they make with a cabin (except maybe the 21.1) and all their center consoles (particularly the 17.1, 21.1, 23.1, and the 24.1 foot versions, which are the newer versions). Even the 17-foot and 18-foot flats have great resale. Hey, if you can find a 26.3 walk-around, grab it.

Maverick/Hewes

Built in Fort Pierce, Florida. Flats boats. Maverick/Hewes invented the flats fishing sport. This innovative company has been building quality flats boats for over 50 years, and you can't beat them when it comes to value and re-sale. The boats are well thought out for their purpose: they float and run shallow, pole easily (with the possible exception of the Light Tackles), and ride very well for a small boat. Even the entry-level boats, such as the 16-foot and 18-foot Bayfisher, excel in quality. I especially like the 19-foot Redfisher. If you can find one, buy it.

Pursuit

Built in Fort Pierce, Florida. Center consoles and walk-around cuddies. Pursuit makes a very nice series of center consoles and walk-around cuddies. These heavily built, deep V hulls ride well and provide superior seating and nice cabins. They could stand to pay a little more attention to fishing amenities (the smaller models could use more fishboxes). These are fairly pricey, but they hold their value well. I like the ride in the 23.5 and 24.70 center console models; my favorite cabin model is the 25.5.

Sea Ray

Built in Knoxville, Tennessee. Bowriders, small cuddies, deckboats, center consoles, larger cruisers, and jet boats. Sea Ray is one of the most respected names in the pleasure boat industry. I like their little bowriders and made a lot of money on their Sevilles, from 17- to 20-foot versions. Then skip up to their mid-sized cruisers. The 23- to 27-foot Sundancers are great. Make sure you get at least a big block V-8 in the 27-footer. Sea Rays offer a great ride, excellent layouts, and solid backing by the manufacturer and dealers. This one is a winner. Some awesome deals can be had on older hulls.

Tiara

Built in Holland, Michigan. Small and larger cruisers. I've never met a Tiara owner who wasn't crazy about his boat. Their cruisers are especially nice: top-quality materials, great ride and handling, nicely appointed, durable, and classy. The 27-foot Continental cruiser model is an all-time favorite. Also very popular are the 27- through 31-foot Opens. If you are lucky enough to find a deal on one of these, take it and run.

World Cat (formerly Sea Cat)

Built in Greenville, North Carolina. Center console and walk-around cuddy catamarans. World Cat is a benchmark among fishing catamarans. Fast and extremely stable, these top quality boats hang on to their resale value tenaciously. They are well thought out for fishing, with huge cockpits and nice cabins. Mount a pair of 4-stroke Yamahas or Hondas and you'll run forever on a tank of gas. The 21-foot or 26-foot versions are both a great catch.

Yamaha

Built in Cypress, California. Personal watercraft and jet boats. I'm not a real jet fan, but these folks are the innovators. If you want speed (and what else are these things good for?), you get Yamaha. Quality, reliability, and speed. Get on a twin-jet Exiter for an exciting ride. Watch the resale, however. Jets always seem to lose you money, so buy inexpensively.

Quality Boat Lines

Aqua Sport

Built in Sarasota, Florida. Center consoles, walk-around cuddies, dual consoles. A good quality boatbuilder, Aqua Sport claims to have invented the center console design. Nothing exceptional here except for a good resale value. The hulls tend to ride a little rough and wet, but they are great fair weather fishing boats. I prefer their smaller center consoles, from 16 to 22 feet. The newer 21-foot walk-around (after 1998) is nice, and the 21-foot dual console

has a great layout. Older hulls are great bay boats and
hold their value well.

Century

*Built in Panama City, Florida. Center consoles, walk-around
cuddies, and dual consoles.* The third-oldest boat manufacturer in the country, Century offers good quality and resale value, and their boats are well built and well backed. I
like their older boats—the smaller bowriders and cuddies
from the mid-1980s to the early 1990s. Formerly in the
pleasure craft industry (runabouts and cruisers), Century
now produces fishing boats exclusively. The company has
great hulls up to 21 feet. The 23- to 30-foot models need
a little more deadrise. But as of this writing, I hear the
company is working on it.

Chris Craft

*Built in Bradenton, Florida. Bowriders, small cuddies, larger
cruisers, center consoles, and walk-around cuddies.* The oldest
boatbuilder in America has taken the opposite tack from
Century and virtually dropped their fishing boat line.
Chris Craft delivers good all-round quality and innovative
layouts. I like their smaller (under 23 feet) bowriders and
cuddies. I also like their old Sea Hawk fishing hulls, the
21- and 23-foot models in particular. The Concept series
has some great use of space, both on deck and down
below. These boats ride well, hold up well, and have good
resale value.

Godfrey/Hurricane

*Built in Elkhart, Indiana (among other sites). Pontoon and
deckboats.* One of the originators of the deckboat craze,
Godfrey/Hurricane is one of the better manufacturers in
this area. The pontoon boats feature marine plywood
decks with a 50-year warranty. (Read this document
carefully: after a short period, they will give you new

plywood and you'll have to do the replacing yourself.)
The 20-footer is a nice size, handles well for a pontoon
boat, and you can carry ten of your closest friends (at
about 10 knots). Make sure pontoons and hardware are
set up for salt water if you are using it there. Resale on
pontoons is never good, so make sure you get a great
deal.

The more recent deckboats boast molded fiberglass decks and seating. Take your closest friends skiing in
this one (with maximum power). In this category, I like
the 22-footer.

Hydra Sport

*Built in Murfreesboro, Tennessee. Center consoles, walk-around
cuddies, and dual consoles.* Hydra Sport is a great boatbuilder, both innovative and conscientious. I've never
heard a discouraging word from their owners. The boats
offer a great ride and are very durable and well thought
out for anglers. I particularly like the 18- to 24-foot center consoles. The Sea Skiff series isn't bad, but these
should be bought at much lower prices than their liner
boats.

Maxum

*Built in Arlington, Washington. Bowriders, small cuddies, and
small and larger cruisers.* Maxum gives you a lot of boat
and features for the money. While some of the hardware
and fittings could be of higher quality, the boats ride
well, have some nice appointments, and come with a
generous package of standard features. I consider these a
step up from their Bayliner cousins (same manufacturer),
and they seem to hold up well over the years with some
minor (hardware) repairs. The resale is all right. There are
some great deals to be had on these hulls. The 19-foot
bowriders are quick, and the 23-foot cuddy is a great all-
round family boat.

Pro-Line

Built in Homosassa, Florida. Center consoles, walk-around cuddies, flats boats, and jet boats. Pro-Line is a builder of consistent quality. I am particularly fond of their walk-around cuddies. They have the nicest cabins that I've seen on a smaller fishing boat. Give me a 21- to 26-foot walk-around and I'm good for the duration. My favorite models are the 211, the 230, and the huge 2510. Pro-Lines offer nice layouts, a decent ride (not the best, but you can't have everything), and quality fittings and hardware. This one's a keeper.

Regal

Built in Orlando, Florida. Bowriders, small cuddies, larger cruisers, deckboats, and jet boats. So many models, so little time. Regal hulls are nicely built, with great layouts and hardware. They hold up well, both physically and in value. I like the smaller boats—17- and 20-foot bowriders, the 24-foot Destiny deckboats, and the bigger cruisers. I dislike the jets; but to be honest, I dislike all jets. These hulls ride well, handle well, and are generally well appointed. Definitely upper class.

Scout

Built in Summersville, South Carolina. Center consoles, flats boats, and dual consoles. Small boats, small company. Scout brings you great quality and innovative hull designs and layouts. Unsinkable as a Whaler, they are designed with the avid fisherman in mind. I like the 16-foot flats, the 17- and 18-foot center consoles, and the 18-foot dual console. The 20-footer is as big as they get for now. It's hard to find. But if you do find one, get it.

Sylvan/Smoker Cat

Built in New Paris, Indiana. Pontoon boats, deckboats and jon boats. Like Godfrey/Hurricane, this is another quality builder in this category. On older pontoons, try to avoid seats made with vinyl-covered wood. Look for Roto Cast (molded plastic) seats. For pontoon boats, Sylvan/ Smoker's boats are well built and durable. I prefer the 20- or 22-foot models. They make a nice 24-foot deckboat with an enclosed head area. Quick, agile, and relatively dry (keep the nose up), they are great party boats.

Wellcraft

Built in Sarasota, Florida. Center consoles, walk-around cuddies, flats boats, bowriders, small and large performance cruisers. I've probably made more money on this boat line than any other. Wellcraft offers good, dependable quality for less. As a group, these boats are smooth riding, stable, durable, and dependable. My favorites are the 18- and 20-foot center consoles, the 23- and 25-foot Sportsman walk-arounds, the newer Coastal series walk-arounds, the 17- to 21-foot bowriders and small cuddies, the 23-foot Aruba, and the larger 32-foot San Tropez cruisers. And let's not forget the Novas and the Scarabs.

Honorable Mentions

As I stated earlier, I am not personally acquainted with all the different manufacturers in the country, and there certainly are many more reputable boatbuilders available. So I briefly give an honorable mention to builders known for their quality with which I have limited experience.

Center Consoles, Flats Boats, Walk-Around Cuddies

- **Action Craft** in Cape Coral, Florida
- **Dusky** in Dania, Florida
- **Intrepid** in Dania, Florida
- **Key West** in Ridgeville, California

- ▣ **Parker** in Beaufort, North Carolina

- ▣ **Robalo/Wahoo** in Arlington, Washington

- ▣ **Shamrock** in Cape Coral, Florida

Bowriders, Small Cuddies, Larger Cruisers

- ▣ **Chaparral** in Nashville, Georgia

- ▣ **Donzi** in Sarasota, Florida

- ▣ **Four Winns** in Cadillac, Michigan

Bass Boats

- ▣ **ProCraft** in Murfreesboro, Tennessee

- ▣ **Ranger** in Kent, Washington

- ▣ **Skeeter** in Kilgore, Texas

- ▣ **Tracker** in Springfield, Missouri

Jet Boats and Personal Watercraft (PWC)

- ▣ **Donzi** in Sarasota, Florida

- ▣ **Kawasaki** in Irvine, California

- ▣ **Sea Doo** in Melborne, Florida

Performance Boats

- ▣ **Baja** in Bucyrus, Ohio

- ▣ **Cigarette** in Miami Beach, Florida

- ▣ **Donzi** in Sarasota, Florida

Catamarans

▣ **Glacier Bay** in Monroe, Washington

▣ **Sea Gull** in Naples, Florida

▣ **Talon** in Sarasota, Florida

Appendix 3

State Boating Authorities

The U.S. Coast Guard website maintains a list of State Boating Law Administrators and officials. Check it for the latest data: <*http://www.uscgboating.org/state1.html*>. This list is alphabetical by state. For information on Canada, call the Canadian Coast Guard at 800-267-6687.

United States

Dept. of Conservation and Natural
  Resources
Marine Police Division
64 N. Union St., Room 438
Montgomery, Alabama 36130-1451
334-242-3673

Alaska Dept. of Natural Resources,
  Division of Parks and Outdoor
  Recreation
3601 C Street, Suite 1280
Anchorage, Alaska 99503-5921
907-269-8705
Fax 907-269-8907

Arizona Game and Fish Dept.
2221 W. Greenway Rd.
Phoenix, Arizona 85023
602-789-3383

Arkansas Game & Fish Commission
Boating Safety Division
2 Natural Resources Dr.
Little Rock, Arkansas 72205
501-223-6399

Dept. of Boating and Waterways
2000 Evergreen St., Suite 100
Sacramento, California 95815
916-263-4327

Division of Parks & Outdoor Recreation
13787 S. Hwy. 85
Littleton, Colorado 80125
303-791-1954

Dept. Marine Headquarters
P.O. Box 280
Old Lyme, Connecticut 06371
860-424-3124

Division of Fish and Wildlife
Richardson and Robbins Bldg.
P.O. Box 1401
Dover, Delaware 19903
302-739-3440

Metropolitan Police Dept.
Harbor Patrol Branch
550 Water St. SW
Washington, D.C. 20024
202-727-4582

Dept. of Environmental Protection
Division of Law Enforcement
3900 Commonwealth Blvd., MS 630
Tallahassee, Florida 32399-3000
850-488-5600

Florida Game, Fresh Water Fish Commission
Division of Law Enforcement
620 South Meridian Street
Tallahassee, Florida 32399-1600
850-488-6257

Dept. of Natural Resources
Wildlife Resources Division

Law Enforcement Section
2070 US Hwy., 278, SE
Social Circle, Georgia 30025
770-918-6408

Dept. of Land and Natural Resources
Division of Boating and Ocean
    Recreation
333 Queen St., Suite 300
Honolulu, Hawaii 96813
808-587-1975

Dept. of Parks and Recreation
P.O. Box 83720
Boise, Idaho 83720-0655
208-334-4180

Dept. of Conservation
Division of Law Enforcement
524 S. Second St.
Springfield, Illinois 62701-1787
217-782-6431

Dept. of Natural Resources
Law Enforcement Division
IGCS, Room W255-D
402 W. Washington
Indianapolis, Indiana 46204
317-232-4010

Dept. of Conservation
Fish and Wildlife Division
Wallace State Office Bldg.
E. 9th and Grand Ave.
Des Moines, Iowa 50319-0034
515-281-8652

Kansas Wildlife and Parks
900 SW Jackson
Topeka, Kansas 66612-1233
913-296-2281

Kentucky Water Patrol
Kentucky Dept. of Fish and Wildlife
    Resources
#1 Game Farm Rd.
Frankfort, Kentucky 40601
502-564-3074

Dept. of Wildlife and Fisheries
P.O. Box 98000
2000 Quail Dr.
Baton Rouge, Louisiana 70898-9000
504-765-2983

Inland Fisheries and Wildlife
284 State St. Section #41
Augusta, Maine 04333
207-287-2766

Dept. of Natural Resources
Tawes State Office Bldg., B-1
580 Taylor Ave.
Annapolis, Maryland 21401
410-260-8881

Division of Environmental Law Enforcement
175 Portland St.
Boston, Massachusetts 02214-1701
617-727-3190

Dept. of Natural Resources
Law Enforcement Division
P.O. Box 30028
Lansing, Michigan 48909
517-335-3416

Dept. of Natural Resources
Attn: Boating Safety
500 Lafayette Rd.
St. Paul, Minnesota 55155
612-296-3336

Dept. of Wildlife, Fisheries and Parks
P.O. Box 451
Jackson, Mississippi 39205
601-364-2185

Missouri State Water Patrol
Dept. of Public Safety
P.O. Box 1368
Jefferson City, Missouri 65102-1368
573-751-3333

Montana Fish, Wildlife and Parks
Enforcement Division
1420 E. 6th Ave.
P.O. Box 200701
Helena, Montana 59620
406-444-2452

Nebraska Game and Parks Commission
Law Enforcement Division
2200 N. 33rd St.
Lincoln, Nebraska 68503-0370
402-471-5579

Dept. of Conservation and Natural
    Resources, Division of Wildlife
1100 Valley Road
P.O. Box 10678
Reno, Nevada 89520-0022
702-688-1542

Division of Safety Services
31 Dock Rd.
Gilford, New Hampshire 03246
603-293-2037

New Jersey State Police
Troop F
P.O. Box 7068
West Trenton, New Jersey 08628-0068
609-882-2000, ext. 6164

Energy, Minerals, and Natural Resources
    Dept.
Parks and Recreation Division
P.O. Box 1147
Santa Fe, New Mexico 87504-1147
505-827-7173

Bureau of Marine and Recreation Vehicles
Agency Bldg. #1, 13th floor
Empire State Plaza
Albany, New York 12238
518-473-0179

Wildlife Resources Commission
512 N. Salsbury St.
Archdale Building
Raleigh, North Carolina 27604-1188
919-733-7191

Game & Fish Dept.
Information & Education Div.
100 N. Bismarck Expressway
Bismarck, North Dakota 58501-5095
701-328-6327

Dept. of Natural Resources
Division of Watercraft
4435 Fountain Square Dr.
Columbus, Ohio 43224-1300
614-265-6485

Lake Patrol Division
Dept. of Public Safety
P.O. Box 11415
Oklahoma City, Oklahoma 73136-0415
405-425-2143

State Marine Board
435 Commercial St., NE
Salem, Oregon 97310
503-373-1405, ext. 244

Pennsylvania Fish & Boat Commission
Bureau of Boating
P.O. Box 67000
Harrisburg, Pennsylvania 17106-7000
717-657-4538

Dept. of Environmental Management
235 Providence Street
Providence, Rhode Island 02908
401-277-3071

Wildlife and Marine Resources Dept.
Division of Law Enforcement & Boating
P.O. Box 12559
Charleston, South Carolina 29412
803-762-5034

Dept. of Game, Fish, and Parks
Div. of Wildlife
523 E. Capitol
Pierre, South Dakota 57501-3182
605-773-4506

Tennessee Wildlife Resources Agency
Boating Division
P.O. Box 40747
Nashville, Tennessee 37204-9979
615-781-6682

Texas Parks and Wildlife Dept.
Law Enforcement Division
4200 Smith School Rd.
Austin, Texas 78744
512-389-4624

Division of Parks & Recreation
1594 W. North Temple Street
P.O. Box 146001
Salt Lake City, Utah 84114-6001
801-538-7341

Vermont State Police HQ
103 S. Main Street
Waterbury, Vermont 05671
802-244-8778

Dept. of Game and Inland Fisheries
P.O. Box 11104
Richmond, Virginia 23230-1104
804-367-1189

Washington State Parks & Recreation
    Commission
P.O. Box 42654
Olympia, Washington 98504-2654
360-902-8525

Division of Natural Resources
Law Enforcement Section
Capital Complex, Bldg 3
Charleston, West Virginia 25305-0668
304-558-2783

Dept. of Natural Resources
Division of Law Enforcement
P.O. Box 7921
Madison, Wisconsin 53707
608-266-2141

Wildlife Law Enforcement
Game and Fish Dept.
5400 Bishop Blvd.
Cheyenne, Wyoming 82006
307-777-4579

U.S. Territories
American Samoa
Department of Special Operations
P.O. Box 1086
Pago Pago, American Samoa 96799
011-684-633-2004

Guam
Guam Police Department
Special Program Section
P.O. Box 23909
GMF Barrigada, Guam 96921

Northern Marinas [CNMI]
Boating and Safety Section
Department of Public Safety
P.O. Box 791
Saipan, CNMI, 96950
011-670 233-7233

Puerto Rico
Office of the Commissioner of Navigation
Dept. of Natural Resources
P.O. Box 5887
Puerta de Tierra, Puerto Rico 00906
787-724-2340

U.S. Virgin Islands
Dept. of Planning and Natural Resources
396-1 Foster Plaza
Annas Retreat
St. Thomas, U.S. Virgin Islands 00802
809-776-8600

Appendix 4

Coast Guard–Required Safety Gear

Boat operators are required to carry a minimum of safety equipment (referred to as "carriage requirements") and comply with federal and state regulations for such things as numbering and operation. The Federal Equipment Requirements are minimum requirements and do not guarantee the safety of the vessel or its passengers. For this reason additional safety equipment is recommended. Minimum federal requirements are printed in *italic*. To meet these standards, in some cases, the equipment must be Coast Guard–approved. Equipment designated as Coast Guard–approved has been determined to be in compliance with U.S. Coast Guard specifications and regulations relating to performance, construction, or materials.

Personal Flotation Devices (PFDs, or life jackets)

All recreational boats must carry one Type I, II, III, or V PFD (wearable) for each person aboard. For Type V PFDs to be counted they must be used according to their label requirements. Any boat 16 feet and longer (except canoes and kayaks) must also carry one Type IV (throwable) PFD.

PFDs must be Coast Guard approved, in good and serviceable condition, and of appropriate size for the intended user. *Wearable PFDs must be readily accessible,* meaning you must be able to put them on in a reasonable amount of time in an emergency (vessel sinking, a fire, etc.). They should not be stowed in plastic bags, in locked or closed compartments, or have other gear stowed on top of them, as specified: *Throwable devices must be immediately available for use.*

Although not required, a PFD should be worn at all times when the vessel is underway. A wearable PFD may save your life—but only if you wear it.

When available, Coast Guard–approved inflatable PFDs will be authorized only for adults.

Types of PFDs

PFDs are classified by type. The following list describes each type's attributes.

☐ **Type I PFD.** A Type I PFD, or offshore life jacket, provides the most buoyancy. It is effective for all waters, especially open, rough, or remote waters where rescue may be delayed. It is designed to turn most unconscious wearers in the water to a face-up position. The Type I comes in two sizes. The adult size provides at least 22 pounds buoyancy; the child size provides at least 11 pounds buoyancy.

☐ **Type II PFD.** A Type II PFD, or near-shore buoyancy vest, is intended for calm, inland water or where there is a good chance of quick rescue. This type will turn *some* unconscious wearers to a face-up position in the water. The turning action is not as pronounced, and it will not turn as many persons to a face-up position under the same conditions as a Type I. An adult size device provides at least 15½ pounds buoyancy; a medium child size provides 11 pounds. Infant and small child sizes each provide at least 7 pounds buoyancy.

Type III PFD. A Type III PFD, or flotation aid, is good for calm, inland water, or where there is a good chance of quick rescue. It is designed so wearers can place themselves in a face-up position in the water. The wearer may have to tilt their head back to avoid turning face-down in the water. The Type III has the same minimum buoyancy as the Type II PFD. It comes in many styles, colors, and sizes and is generally the most comfortable type for continuous wear. Float coats, fishing vests, and vests designed with features suitable for various sports activities are examples of this type of PFD.

Type IV PFD. A Type IV PFD, or throwable device, is intended for calm, inland water with heavy boat traffic where help is always present. It is designed to be thrown to a person in the water and grasped and held by the user until he or she is rescued. It is not designed to be worn. Type IV devices include buoyant cushions, ring buoys, and horseshoe buoys.

Type V PFD. A Type V PFD, or special use device, is intended for specific activities and may be carried instead of another PFD *only if used according to the approval condition on that label.* Some Type V devices provide significant hypothermia protection. Varieties include deck suits, work vests, boardsailing vests, and hybrid PFDs.

Type V Hybrid Inflatable PFD. This is the least bulky of all PFD types. It contains a small amount of inherent buoyancy and an inflatable chamber. Its performance is equal to a Type I,

II, or III PFD (as noted on the PFD label) when inflated. *Hybrid PFDs must be worn when underway to be acceptable.*

Child PFD Requirements

Some states require that PFDs be worn by children of specific ages under certain conditions. Check with your state boating safety officials (see appendix 3). Federal law does not require PFDs on racing shells, rowing sculls, and racing kayaks. State laws can vary.

Remember, PFDs will keep you from sinking— but not necessarily from drowning. Extra time should be taken in selecting a properly sized PFD to insure a safe fit. Testing your PFD in shallow water or in a guarded swimming pool is a good and reassuring practice.

Water Skiing, Personal Watercraft, and PFDs

A water skier is considered on board the vessel and a PFD is required for the purposes of compliance with the PFD carriage requirements. It is advisable and recommended for skiers and personal watercraft (PWC) riders to wear a PFD designed to withstand the impact of hitting the water at high speed. The "impact class" marking on the label refers to PFD strength, not personal protection. Most states require skiers and PWC riders to wear PFDs while underway.

Visual Distress Signals

All vessels used on coastal waters, the Great Lakes, territorial seas, and those waters connected directly to them, up to a point where a body of water is less than two miles wide, must be equipped with U.S.C.G.–approved visual distress signals. Vessels owned in the United States operating on the high seas must be equipped with U.S.C.G.–approved visual distress signals. The following vessels are not required to carry day signals, but they must carry night signals when operating from sunset to sunrise.

🔲 Recreational boats less than 16 feet in length

🔲 Boats participating in organized events, such as races or regattas or marine parades.

🔲 Open sailboats less than 26 feet in length not equipped with propulsion machinery

🔲 Manually propelled boats

Regulations prohibit display of visual distress signals on the water under any circumstances except when assistance is required to prevent immediate or potential danger to persons on board a vessel.

Pyrotechnic Devices

Pyrotechnic Visual Distress Signals must be Coast Guard–approved, in serviceable condition, and readily accessible. They are marked with a date showing the service life, which must not have expired. Launchers manufactured before January 1, 1981, intended for use with approved signals, are not required to be Coast Guard approved. If pyrotechnic devices are selected, a minimum of three are required. That is, three signals for day use and three signals for night. Some pyrotechnic signals meet both day and night use requirements. Pyrotechnic devices should be stored in a cool, dry location. A watertight container painted red or orange and prominently marked "Distress Signals" is recommended.

Coast Guard–approved pyrotechnic distress signals and associated devices include

🔲 Pyrotechnic red flares, hand-held or aerial

🔲 Pyrotechnic orange smoke, hand-held or floating

🔲 Launchers for aerial red meteors or parachute flares

Non-Pyrotechnic Devices

Non-Pyrotechnic Visual Distress Signals must be in serviceable condition, readily accessible, and certified by the manufacturer as complying with U.S.C.G. requirements. They include

☐ Orange distress flag

☐ Electric distress light

The distress flag is a day signal only. It must be at least 3 feet by 3 feet with a black square and ball on an orange background. It is most distinctive when attached and waved on a paddle, boathook, or flown from a mast.

The electric distress light is accepted for night use only and must automatically flash the international SOS distress signal.

Under Inland Navigation Rules, a high intensity white light flashing at regular intervals from 50 to 70 times per minute is considered a distress signal.

Fire Extinguishers

Coast Guard–approved fire extinguishers are required on certain boats. . . . Motorboats are required to carry fire extinguishers if any one or more of the following conditions exist.

☐ Inboard engines.

☐ Closed compartments and compartments under seats where portable fuel tanks may be stored.

☐ Double bottoms not sealed to the hull or not completely filled with flotation materials.

☐ Closed living spaces.

☐ Closed stowage compartments in which combustible or flammable materials are stored.

▣ **Permanently installed fuel tanks.** Fuel tanks secured so they cannot be moved in case of fire or other emergency are considered permanently installed. There are no gallon capacity limits to determine if a fuel tank is portable. If the weight of a fuel tank is such that persons on board cannot move it, the Coast Guard considers it permanently installed.

Extinguishers are classified by a letter and number symbol. The letter indicates the type of fire the unit is designed to extinguish (for example, Type B extinguishers are designed to extinguish flammable liquids such as gasoline, oil, and grease fires). The number indicates the relative size of the extinguisher (the minimum extinguishing agent weight).

Classes	Foam (gals.)	Dry CO_2 (lbs.)	Chemical (lbs.)	Halon (lbs.)
B-I	1.25	4	2	2.5
B-II	2.5	1.5	10	10

Minimum Number of Hand-Portable Fire Extinguishers Required		
Vessel Length	No Fixed System	With Approved Fixed Systems
Less than 26′	1 B-I	0
26′ to less than 40′	2 B-I or 1 B-II	1 B-I
40′ to 65′	3 B-I or 1 B-II and 1 B-I	2 B-I or 1 B-II

Coast Guard–approved extinguishers are hand portable, either B-I or B-II classification, and have a specific marine-type mounting bracket. It is recommended that extinguishers be mounted in a readily accessible position.

Ventilation

All boats that use gasoline for electrical generation, mechanical power or propulsion are required to be equipped with a ventilation system.

A "natural" ventilation system is required for each compartment in a boat that

- ▣ contains a permanently installed gasoline engine
- ▣ has openings between it and a compartment that requires ventilation
- ▣ contains a permanently installed fuel tank and an electrical component that is not ignition-protected
- ▣ contains a fuel tank that vents into that compartment (including a portable tank)
- ▣ contains a nonmetallic fuel tank

A natural ventilation system consists of a supply opening or duct from the atmosphere (located on the exterior surface of the boat), from a ventilated compartment, or from a compartment that is open to the atmosphere, and an exhaust opening into another ventilated compartment or an exhaust duct to the atmosphere.

Each exhaust opening or exhaust duct must originate in the lower one-third of the compartment. Each supply opening or supply duct and each exhaust opening or duct in a compartment must be above the normal accumulation of bilge water.

A "powered" ventilation system is required for each compartment in a boat that has a permanently installed gasoline engine with a cranking motor for remote starting.

A powered ventilation system consists of one or more exhaust blowers. Each intake duct for an exhaust blower must be in the lower one-third of the compartment and above the normal accumulation of bilge water.

For boats built prior to 1980, there was no requirement for a powered ventilation system; however, some boats were equipped with a blower.

Manufacturers of boats built after 1980 with remote starters are required to display a label which contains the following information:

Warning

Gasoline vapors can explode. Before starting engine, operate blower at least 4 minutes and check engine compartment bilge for gasoline vapors.

All owners of boats equipped with exhaust blowers are strongly encouraged to take the same precautions before starting a gasoline engine.

All owners are responsible for keeping their boat's ventilation systems in operating condition. This means making sure openings are free of obstructions, ducts are not blocked or torn, blowers operate properly, and worn components are replaced with equivalent marine-type equipment.

Backfire Flame Control

Gasoline engines installed in a vessel after April 25, 1940 (except outboard motors) must be equipped with an acceptable means of backfire flame control. The device must be suitably attached to the air intake with a flame tight connection and is required to be Coast Guard–approved or comply with SAE J-1928 or UL 1111 standards and marked accordingly.

Sound Producing Devices

The U.S. Coast Guard Navigation Rules, International-Inland, require sound signals to be made under certain circumstances. Meeting, crossing, and overtaking situations described in the Navigation Rules are examples of when sound signals are required. Recreational vessels are also required to sound signals during periods of reduced visibility.

Vessels 12 meters or more in length are required to carry on board a whistle or horn, and a bell. Any vessel less than 12 meters (39.4 feet) in length is required to make an efficient sound signal to signal its intentions and to signal its position in periods of reduced visibility. Vessels under 12 meters may carry a whistle or horn to do so.

Consult the Navigation Rules, International-Inland, or a publication that summarizes them, for specific information on sound signals.

Navigation Lights

The U.S. Coast Guard Navigation Rules, International-Inland, require vessels to display lights and shapes under certain conditions. *Recreational vessels are required to display navigation lights between sunset and sunrise and other periods of reduced visibility* (such as fog, rain or haze). For example, a power-driven vessel less than 12 meters (39.4 feet) in length might show a white masthead (forward) light visible for 2 miles, a white stern light visible for 2 miles, and separate red and green side lights visible for 1 mile. The same boat could also opt for a single all-around white light, visible for 2 miles, and combined sidelights visible for 1 mile. The masthead or all-around white light on power vessels less than 12 meters in length must be at least 1 meter above the red and green side lights.

Consult the Navigation Rules, International-Inland, or a publication that summarizes them, for specific information on the placement and characteristics of lights.

Shapes and Lights

To alert other vessels to conditions that may be hazardous, there are requirements to display lights at night and shapes during the day. At night, for example, vessels at anchor must often display anchor lights. An anchor light for a vessel less than 50 meters (164 feet) in length is an all-around white light visible for 2 miles exhibited where it can best be seen. During the day, vessels at anchor are required to exhibit a ball shape forward, where it can best be seen. Vessels under 20 meters (65.6 feet) long are not required to display anchoring lights or shapes if they are anchored in a designated anchorage area, such as those found near marinas. Vessels under 7 meters (23 feet) long are not required to display anchor lights or dayshapes unless anchored in or near a narrow channel, fairway, or anchorage, or where other vessels normally navigate.

Consult the Navigation Rules, International-Inland, or a publication that summarizes them, for specific information on the display of shapes and lights.

Recommended Equipment

Besides meeting the legal requirements, prudent boaters carry additional safety equipment. The following list of additional items of equipment is suggested—depending on the size, location, and use of your boat. You may want to carry

- charts and compass
- VHF radio
- dewatering device (pump or bailer)
- alternate propulsion (paddles)
- whistle or horn
- visual distress signals

- fuel tanks
- spare fuel
- anchor
- spare anchor
- spare propeller
- heaving line
- ring buoy
- mooring line
- fenders
- searchlight
- binoculars
- flashlight

- spare batteries
- boat hook
- first-aid kit
- food and water
- mirror
- sunglasses
- sunburn lotion
- marine hardware
- extra clothing
- tool kit
- spare parts

This information was compiled from the U.S. Coast Guard website, <http://www.uscgboating.org/pubs.html>.

Index